AN ALL-SURPASSING
FELLOWSHIP

AN ALL-SURPASSING
FELLOWSHIP

*Learning from Robert Murray M'Cheyne's
Communion with God*

David P. Beaty

REFORMATION HERITAGE BOOKS
Grand Rapids, Michigan

An All-Surpassing Fellowship
© 2014 by David P. Beaty

Reformation Heritage Books
2965 Leonard St. NE
Grand Rapids, MI 49525
616-977-0889 / Fax 616-285-3246
orders@heritagebooks.org
www.heritagebooks.org

All royalties from the sale of this book support Buildministry.org, an equipping ministry of River Oaks Community Church. Buildministry.org provides free biblical training resources to church leaders around the world.

Printed in the United States of America
14 15 16 17 18 19/10 9 8 7 6 5 4 3 2 1

Library of Congress Cataloging-in-Publication Data

Beaty, David P.
  An all-surpassing fellowship : learning from Robert Murray M'Cheyne's communion with God / David P. Beaty.
     pages cm
  Includes bibliographical references.
  ISBN 978-1-60178-315-8 (pbk. : alk. paper) 1. M'Cheyne, Robert Murray, 1813-1843. 2. Presbyterian Church—Scotland—Clergy—Religious life. 3. Church of Scotland—Clergy—Religious life. 4. Spiritual life—Presbyterian Church. 5. Spiritual life—Church of Scotland. I. Title.
  BX9225.M17B43 2014
  285'.2092—dc23
  [B]
                                        2014010034

For additional Reformed literature, request a free book list from Reformation Heritage Books at the above regular or e-mail address.

To
Beth, Anna, and Matthew

Contents

————— ❦ —————

Introduction

⟡

Chosen not for good in me,
Wakened up from wrath to flee,
Hidden in the Saviour's side,
By the Spirit sanctified.
Teach me, Lord, on earth to show,
By my love, how much I owe.

—Robert Murray M'Cheyne, *Memoir and
Remains of Robert Murray M'Cheyne*

Robert Murray M'Cheyne died when he was only twenty-nine years old. His death ended his flourishing pastoral and evangelistic ministry only seven years after he began preaching in the Church of Scotland. But the brevity of his life and ministry stand in contrast to his enduring influence. Just one year after M'Cheyne's death in 1843, his closest friend, Andrew Bonar, completed the *Memoir and Remains of Robert Murray M'Cheyne*. By 1910, approximately half a million copies of this record of M'Cheyne's life were in circulation around the world. Countless Christian leaders have been influenced by Bonar's account of his friend. Renowned preacher C. H. Spurgeon described the memoir as "one of the best and most profitable volumes ever published."[1] Theologian

---

1. Andrew A. Bonar, *Memoir and Remains of Robert Murray M'Cheyne* (1844; repr., Edinburgh: Banner of Truth, 2004), cover.

D. A. Carson has described M'Cheyne as one of the "Overlooked Shapers of Evangelicalism."[2]

M'Cheyne's influence did not come about because of the revival that shook both the church he pastored and his country of Scotland. Nor has it continued primarily because of his biblical, evangelistic sermons. Rather, M'Cheyne's enduring influence flows from the depth and vibrancy of his walk with God. His love for Jesus Christ overflowed in a life of holiness and humility that was evident to those who knew him or heard him preach. "He was the meekest, calmest, and holiest believer that ever I saw," wrote one who knew him.[3] M'Cheyne's friend Robert Macdonald wrote:

> Mr. McCheyne's holiness was noticeable even before he spoke a word; his appearance spoke for him. There was a minister in the north of Scotland with whom he spent a night. He was so marvelously struck by this about him, that when Mr. McCheyne left the room, he burst into tears and said, "O, that is the most Jesus-like man I ever saw." Robert McCheyne would sometimes say but one word, or quote a text; but it was blessed. I never got even a note from him that I could burn. There was always something in it worth keeping; God seemed to bless all he wrote.[4]

In his memoir of M'Cheyne, Bonar records a tribute written by a Mr. Hamilton of London. The tribute includes this observation of M'Cheyne's life: "A striking characteristic of his piety was absorbing love to the Lord Jesus. This was his ruling passion." Hamilton also wrote, "More than any one whom we have ever known, had he learned to do everything in the name of the Lord Jesus."[5]

How did one so young attain such a depth of spiritual maturity and holiness in his few years on earth? Friends and biographers

---

2. David F. Haslam, "Robert Murray M'Cheyne (1813–1843), www.mcheyne .info/rmm.pdf, 1.

3. Alexander Smellie, *Robert Murray M'Cheyne* (1913; repr., Geanies House, Scotland: Christian Focus, 1995), 172.

4. Smellie, *Robert Murray M'Cheyne*, 174–75.

5. A. Bonar, *Memoir and Remains*, 172.

agree that the key to M'Cheyne's spiritual vitality and influence was his devotional life. M'Cheyne considered his communion with God to be "an all-surpassing fellowship" that was foundational to his life and ministry. Andrew Bonar wrote, "With him, the commencement of all labour invariably consisted in the preparation of his own soul. The forerunner of each day's visitations was a calm season of private devotion during morning hours."[6] Bonar also records of M'Cheyne that "his heart was filled and his lips then spoke what he felt within his heart. He gave out not merely living water, but living water drawn at the springs that he himself had drunk of."[7]

Jesus described the work of the Holy Spirit in a believer's life by saying, "Out of his heart will flow rivers of living water" (John 7:38). The truth of Jesus' promise was seen in M'Cheyne's life to an exceptional degree. His close communion with God overflowed with much spiritual life for others. His time alone with God seemed to bring "rivers of living water" to many, as evidenced by M'Cheyne's effectiveness in evangelism and in the revival that came to his church.

As we examine M'Cheyne's communion with God, we will consider his prayer life, his Bible study, and his purposeful pursuit of holiness. We will observe his deep humility, and see its importance in his spiritual maturity. We will seek to understand the vital role of the Holy Spirit in M'Cheyne's walk with God. We will explore these things with a view toward application—to learn from M'Cheyne the attitudes and actions that can help us walk more closely with Christ.

The first section of this work will be an overview of M'Cheyne's life to help us get to know this remarkable Scottish pastor. The second section will focus specifically on his communion with God. In the final section, we will seek to learn from M'Cheyne lessons we can apply to our own lives.

---

6. A. Bonar, *Memoir and Remains*, 34–35.
7. A. Bonar, *Memoir and Remains*, 40.

My prayer is that God will be glorified in this work by increasing our desire for close communion with Him. May He enable us to love Him with all of our hearts and all of our souls and all of our minds (Matt. 22:37). May He cause "rivers of living water" to flow from us to reach a thirsty world.

PART 1

Robert Murray M'Cheyne

Chapter 1

———————— ❧❧ ————————

M'Cheyne's Early Life and Preparation for Ministry

Robert Murray M'Cheyne was born on May 21, 1813, at the family home on 14 Dublin Street in Edinburgh, Scotland. He was the youngest of five children, with two brothers and one sister alive at the time of his birth. He never met his sister Isabella, who died in 1811 when she was nine months old.

M'Cheyne's family was fairly well-off. His father, Adam, was a member of a judicial board charged with drafting ordinances for the Court of Session, the highest judicial body of Scotland. Adam was known as a firm disciplinarian but also as a man who was respected and loved by his children. His mother, whose maiden name was Lockhart Murray Dickson, was known for her warmth and sweet disposition.

Regarding the spiritual atmosphere of the M'Cheyne home, historian Marcus Loane writes, "Both father and mother sought to order the steps of their children in the footprints of the divine Shepherd, and it is clear that their spiritual welfare was fostered from childhood."[1] M'Cheyne's parents attended church regularly, and there the children were taught Scripture and the Westminster Shorter Catechism.[2]

——————————————

1. Marcus L. Loane, *They Were Pilgrims* (Edinburgh: Banner of Truth, 2006), 139.

2. *The Westminster Confession of Faith* (Richmond, Va.: John Knox, 1963).

The M'Cheynes also saw to the intellectual development of their children. When M'Cheyne was only four years old and was recovering from an illness, his father taught him the Greek alphabet. He was able to write the letters on his slate at this early age. A year later, he was sent to his first school. He was a bright student and was noticed for his skills in recitation and singing. About age thirteen, he began to show talent for composing poetry. This gift would become a unique instrument by which he would communicate the gospel in later years.

At the age of fourteen, M'Cheyne was enrolled in the University of Edinburgh, where he completed his arts degree four years later in the spring of 1831. About this time, his family experienced the tragic loss of their son and brother David, and this deeply impacted his life. He had been close to all his siblings—David, Eliza, and William. But it was David, his oldest brother, who had the greatest influence on his life during his childhood. David was eight years older than he, but they spent hours playing games together and shared a mutual interest in writing poetry. David had tutored him in academics and was held in high regard by his younger brother.

But David's most enduring influence on his brother was due to his faith in Jesus Christ. Andrew Bonar writes that in David, "the light of divine grace shone before men with rare and solemn loveliness."[3] David had prayed fervently for his younger brother and had pointed him to the Bible. In his biography of M'Cheyne, Leen J. Van Valen shares M'Cheyne's remembrance about his brother: "He gave me a Bible, and persuaded me to read it"; and "Many a time, I well remember, I have seen him reading his Bible, or shutting his closet door to pray, when I have been dressing to go to some frolic or some dance of folly."[4] When David died from

3. Andrew A. Bonar, *Memoir and Remains of Robert Murray M'Cheyne* (1844; repr., Edinburgh: Banner of Truth, 2004), 6.

4. Leen J. Van Valen, *Constrained by His Love: A New Biography on Robert Murray McCheyne*, trans. Laurence R. Noculson (Geanies House, Scotland: Christian Focus, 2002), 48.

a prolonged illness on July 8, 1831, the entire family was shaken. But for M'Cheyne, the grievous pain of his brother's death became a pathway toward life.

Andrew Bonar writes of M'Cheyne, "He was in his eighteenth year when his brother died; and if this was not the year of his new birth, at least it was the year when the first streaks of dawn appeared in his soul."[5] He always remembered the significance of the date of David's death. On July 8, 1832, he wrote in his diary, "On this morning last year came the first overwhelming blow to my worldliness; how blessed to me, Thou, O God, only knowest, who hast made it so."[6] In a letter to a friend dated July 8, 1842, M'Cheyne wrote, "This day eleven years ago I lost my loved and loving brother, and began to seek a Brother who cannot die."[7]

We might reasonably wonder why M'Cheyne had not come to saving faith earlier in his life. He had been taken to church by his parents and had been taught the catechism and doctrines of Christianity. His life as a child had been exemplary. His own father noted his exceptional behavior: "I never found him guilty of a lie, or of any mean or unworthy action; and he had a great contempt for such things in others. I hardly recollect an instance of my having to inflict personal chastisement upon him."[8] But while his outward life was admirable, his heart was still in need of the righteousness that only Christ can bring. Van Valen helps explain this by asserting that "Robert, as well as his parents, had been moulded by the Enlightenment thinking, which dominated religious life at that time. Sin was considered to be a mere mistake, rather than constituting one guilty before God."[9]

David's death was used by the Holy Spirit to help bring M'Cheyne to an awareness of his sinfulness and his need for the

---

5. A. Bonar, *Memoir and Remains*, 10.
6. A. Bonar, *Memoir and Remains*, 10.
7. Alexander Smellie, *Robert Murray M'Cheyne* (1913; repr., Geanies House, Scotland: Christian Focus, 1995), 37.
8. Smellie, *Robert Murray M'Cheyne*, 33.
9. Van Valen, *Constrained by His Love*, 26.

righteousness of Jesus Christ. As he grew in faith, he increasingly saw the beauty of the righteousness of Christ given to believers. Perhaps his earlier years spent in self-righteousness made him especially sensitive to the deceptive power of trusting in one's own goodness. This awareness of the infinite chasm between human righteousness and the righteousness of Christ marked his preaching for the rest of his life.

His own testimony is perhaps best told in this poem, which he composed on November 18, 1834.[10] The title, "Jehovah Tsidkenu," means "The Lord Our Righteousness," and M'Cheyne notes that this was "the watchword of the Reformers."

> I once was a stranger to grace and to God,
> I knew not my danger, and felt not my load;
> Though friends spoke in rapture of Christ on the tree,
> Jehovah Tsidkenu was nothing to me.
>
> I oft read with pleasure, to soothe or engage,
> Isaiah's wild measure and John's simple page;
> But e'en when they pictured the blood-sprinkled tree
> Jehovah Tsidkenu seemed nothing to me.
>
> Like tears from the daughters of Zion that roll,
> I wept when the waters went over His soul;
> Yet thought not that my sins had nailed to the tree
> Jehovah Tsidkenu—'twas nothing to me.
>
> When free grace awoke me, by light from on high,
> Then legal fears shook me, I trembled to die;
> No refuge, no safety in self could I see—
> Jehovah Tsidkenu my Saviour must be.
>
> My terrors all vanished before the sweet name;
> My guilty fears banished, with boldness I came
> To drink at the fountain, life-giving and free—
> Jehovah Tsidkenu is all things to me.

---

10. A. Bonar, *Memoir and Remains*, 632–33.

Jehovah Tsidkenu! my treasure and boast,
Jehovah Tsidkenu! I ne'er can be lost;
In thee I shall conquer by flood and by field—
My cable, my anchor, my breastplate and shield!

Even treading the valley, the shadow of death,
This "watchword" shall rally my faltering breath;
For while from life's fever my God sets me free,
Jehovah Tsidkenu my death-song shall be.

Preparation for Ministry

In November 1831, just months after his brother's death, M'Cheyne enrolled as a student at the Divinity Hall of Edinburgh University. Here he read *The Sum of Saving Knowledge*,[11] a brief summary of Christian doctrine, which was often appended to the Westminster Confession of Faith at that time. This brought him to a clearer understanding of his acceptance with God through faith in Jesus Christ. A later rereading of the document on March 11, 1834, moved him to write these words in his diary: "Read in the *Sum of Saving Knowledge*, the work which I think first of all wrought a saving change in me. How gladly would I renew the reading of it if that change might be carried on to perfection!"[12]

While a student at Divinity Hall, M'Cheyne also became fluent in Hebrew, the language of the Old Testament. Alexander Smellie writes, "He could consult the Hebrew of the Old Testament, as Bonar testifies, as easily as many ministers consult the Greek of the New. It was not merely the student's enthusiasm for the mastery of his textbook. It was the child's craving for the bread from the Father's table."[13] His love for the study of Scripture in its original language is revealed in a diary entry made during his time at Divinity Hall: "March 6.—Wild wind and rain all day long. Hebrew class—Psalms. New beauty in the original every

---

11. David Dickson and James Durham, *The Sum of Saving Knowledge* (Edinburgh: T. & T. Clark, 1886).
12. A. Bonar, *Memoir and Remains*, 12–13.
13. Smellie, *Robert Murray M'Cheyne*, 40.

time I read."[14] Undoubtedly, M'Cheyne's love of ancient Hebrew was connected with his growing love for the Jews and his desire to see them embrace the Messiah. His facility with the language would help him in later years during his mission to Israel.

M'Cheyne's study at Divinity Hall was marked by an increasing commitment to use his time on earth for God's glory. After spending an evening too carelessly, he wrote in his diary: "Dec. 18—My heart must break off from all these things. What right have I to steal and abuse my Master's time? 'Redeem it,' He is crying to me."[15] Alexander Smellie cites a portion of a letter M'Cheyne sent to his brother in India with a similar emphasis: "Time hastens forward; and this world, like this sheet, will soon be done." Smellie explains, "It was the admonition which constrained him to devote his own feet and hands and brain and heart to a consecration, a labour, and a sacrifice which never were intermitted or relaxed."[16]

M'Cheyne's desire to glorify God with his life was undoubtedly shaped by his reading of Jonathan Edwards. His diary records: "March 20.—…Read part of the Life of Jonathan Edwards. How feeble does my spark of Christianity appear beside such a sun! But even his was a borrowed light, and the same source is still open to enlighten me."[17] Later entries reveal that he bought Edwards's works and continued to study them. The writings and biographies of devoted Christian leaders shaped M'Cheyne during his education and throughout his life. Reading of missionaries like Henry Martyn and David Brainerd helped to form his passion for world missions. The works of men like John Calvin and Jonathan Edwards helped to lay a solid foundation for his theological views. Samuel Rutherford's *Letters* taught him of the "love and loveliness of Christ."[18]

---

14. A. Bonar, *Memoir and Remains*, 143.
15. A. Bonar, *Memoir and Remains*, 14.
16. Smellie, *Robert Murray M'Cheyne*, 41.
17. A. Bonar, *Memoir and Remains*, 15–16.
18. William G. Blaikie, *The Preachers of Scotland: From the Sixth to the Nineteenth Century* (1888; repr., Edinburgh: Banner of Truth, 2001), 114.

His professors at Divinity Hall also helped to shape his future ministry. David Welsh taught church history, and he meant a great deal to M'Cheyne. Welsh was a humble man who showed genuine care for the spiritual development of his students. Each Saturday, he devoted an hour to praying for them.[19] But the professor who had the greatest influence on M'Cheyne was Dr. Thomas Chalmers. In earlier years, Chalmers had been a professing Christian without a true devotion to Jesus Christ. But his life began to change when he faced the death of his favorite sister and then the loss of his beloved uncle. Soon, Chalmers's own life hung in the balance after he contracted a serious illness. It was then that he began to realize that he "recklessly thought not of the greatness of eternity."[20] Gradually, the way of salvation through faith in Jesus Christ became clear to him. He began to memorize Scripture with earnestness and to find joy in prayer. Former religious associates mocked his newfound faith and nicknamed him "mad Chalmers," but he found a new home among those of evangelical faith.[21]

Chalmers soon became a preacher with great influence in Scotland. Yet despite his popularity as a parish pastor, Chalmers felt he could have more usefulness for God's kingdom in the field of education. In 1827, he accepted a professorship of divinity in Edinburgh. When M'Cheyne arrived in 1831, Dr. Chalmers was at the height of his popularity.

Iain Murray has summarized the four key ideas that Chalmers set forth in honing his students for ministry:

1. The governing principle upon which the strength of all ministerial duties depends is regard for the approval of God.

2. Ministers should never rest satisfied without growth in holiness of life.

---

19. Van Valen, *Constrained by His Love*, 79.

20. Iain H. Murray, *A Scottish Christian Heritage* (Edinburgh: Banner of Truth, 2006), 83.

21. Murray, *A Scottish Christian Heritage*, 84.

3. Ministers must give themselves wholly to their true work: Be assured that a single and undivided attention to the peculiar work of a Christian minister is the way of peace and pleasantness.

4. A minister must deal directly with men concerning their need of salvation.[22]

Regarding the fourth idea, Chalmers taught his students what he called "the aggressive principle," that they must pursue the people where they were to be found. This was to be done with house-to-house visitation, including the maintaining of accurate records about the visits.[23]

M'Cheyne soon joined the "Visiting Society," twelve to twenty students who would meet on Saturday mornings for prayer and visitation. The students traveled in pairs to visit the poorest districts of the city, and he was shocked by the needs of the mass of poor people in the city. But these experiences in visitation would prepare him well for his future pastoral ministry.

In addition to learning under the influence of books and professors, M'Cheyne experienced the joy of fellowship with like-minded friends during his preparation for ministry. These included his childhood friend, Alexander Somerville, and Andrew and Horatius Bonar. These men prayed and studied together and learned about the spiritual awakenings of earlier periods. They would each see remarkable workings of God's Spirit in the years to come.

---

22. Murray, *A Scottish Christian Heritage*, 94–96.
23. Murray, *A Scottish Christian Heritage*, 96.

Chapter 2

Pastoral Ministry

On March 29, 1835, M'Cheyne finished his ministerial training in Edinburgh. During April and May of that year, he preached three trial sermons before the Presbytery of Annan, and on July 1, he was officially licensed by it to preach the gospel. His summary of the process and his feelings upon being licensed are expressed in his diary entry on the evening of July 1:

> Preached three probationary discourses in Annan Church, and, after an examination in Hebrew, was solemnly licensed to preach the gospel by Mr. Monylaws, the moderator. "Bless the Lord, O my soul; and all that is within me, be stirred up to praise and magnify His holy name!" What I have so long desired as the highest honour of man, Thou at length givest me—me who dare scarcely use the words of Paul: "Unto me who am less than the least of all saints is this grace given, that I should preach the unsearchable riches of Christ." Felt somewhat solemnised though unable to feel my unworthiness as I ought. Be clothed with humility.[1]

His sense of gratitude for the privilege of preaching the gospel was joined with an awareness of the need for deep humility on the part of those who preach. This quest for humility would continue throughout his ministry.

---

1. Andrew A. Bonar, *Memoir and Remains of Robert Murray M'Cheyne* (1844; repr., Edinburgh: Banner of Truth, 2004), 32–33.

M'Cheyne preached in several churches until November
1835. On November 7, he began as an assistant minister to Rev.
John Bonar in the united parishes of Larbert and Dunipace. Larbert was a town of miners and iron workers, and Dunipace was a
quiet hamlet of farmers. There was a church in each parish, and
M'Cheyne would preach in each on alternate Sundays. During the
week, he was responsible for visiting among the approximately six
thousand residents of the parishes. Regarding this time, Marcus
Loane writes, "Here the groundwork was laid for his future greatness in the pastoral ministry, for his was the heart of a shepherd
who yearned over all who were lost or out of the way."[2] True to his
training under Thomas Chalmers, M'Cheyne was tireless in his
home visitations and kept detailed records of his visits. Here are a
few entries from a notebook he kept of his visits:

> Alexander Hunter, No. 39. Intelligent man. Met with wife in
> Robert's (No. 20). Decent-like family; boy and girl; have lost
> three, spoke of Davy's lamp. Visit, 21 July. *Treasure hid.* He
> recommended prayers for the workers underground.

> Widow Hunter, No. 40. Wicked face, but old body has had
> much trouble. Daughter lame. Visit, 21 July. *Lost sheep.* Spoke
> plain. She spoke grateful things, but felt them not. Invited
> me not to pass the door.

> Peter Rae, No. 44, Ill-looking man. Hard, hard woman. A
> large family of mocking lasses. Visit, July 21. *One thing need-
> ful*, pardon and new heart. Tried to break this northern iron.[3]

The frankness of M'Cheyne's notebook entries should not
obscure the fact that he went about his visits with a prayerful
dependence on the Lord. Concerning his priorities, M'Cheyne
wrote, "I feel it is far better to begin with God—to see His face

---

2. Marcus L. Loane, *They Were Pilgrims* (Edinburgh: Banner of Truth,
2006), 147.

3. Alexander Smellie, *Robert Murray M'Cheyne* (1913; repr., Geanies House,
Scotland: Christian Focus, 1995), 49. The words in italics refer to Scripture passages that he read and explained. They appear in red ink in his notebooks.

first—to get my soul near Him before it is near another."[4] Though ever diligent in his work of visitation and preaching, M'Cheyne realized that fruit was borne by God's work and not merely his own. Therefore, he always sought to draw strength from fellowship with God before ministering to others.

It was while serving as an assistant minister in Larbert and Dunipace that M'Cheyne began to suffer the physical ailments that would continue throughout his life. He began having pain in his chest, accompanied by a nagging cough. A doctor diagnosed the beginnings of tuberculosis and determined that his right lung hardly functioned. The affliction forced him to withdraw from preaching and visitation for a time. But while laid aside from public ministry, he undertook the ministry of intercessory prayer. He wrote to his senior minister, John Bonar, with these words, "I feel distinctly that the whole of my labour during this season of sickness and pain should be in the way of prayer and intercession."[5] Concerning two of the sick people in their parish, M'Cheyne wrote to Bonar, "Poor A. D. and C. H., I often think of them. I can do no more for their good, except pray for them. Tell them that I do this without ceasing."[6]

M'Cheyne was able to return to his ministry duties in Larbert and Dunipace in January 1836. In addition to his ministry of home visitation and prayer, his ministry of preaching began to take shape as well. From the start, M'Cheyne disliked reading his sermons. He would carefully write them out but then commit them to memory as best he could. One morning as he rode his beloved pony, Tully, to Dunipace, his sermon notes were dropped. When he arrived at the church and discovered the loss, he had to preach without his notes. He discovered that he preached with greater freedom and composure than he previously believed he could. While this discovery would not lessen his commitment

---

4. A. Bonar, *Memoir and Remains*, 157.

5. A. Bonar, *Memoir and Remains*, 38.

6. A. Bonar, *Memoir and Remains*, 37.

to study and preparation, it would increase his dependence upon God's Spirit when preaching. He later wrote, "One thing always fills the cup of my consolation, that God may work by the meanest and poorest words, as well as by the most polished and ornate— yea, perhaps more readily, that the glory may be all His own."[7]

As his ministry of preaching developed, M'Cheyne learned the necessity of preparing in prayer as well as study. His diary entry on Sunday, February 21, 1836, reads, "Preached twice in Larbert on the righteousness of God, Rom. i.16. In the morning was more engaged in preparing the head than the heart. This has been frequently my error, and I have always felt the evil of it, especially in prayer. Reform it, then, O Lord." Two weeks later, on March 5, his diary entry reads, "Preached in Larbert with very much comfort, owing chiefly to my remedying the error of 21 Feb. Therefore the heart and the mouth were full. 'Enlarge my heart, and I shall preach.'"[8]

M'Cheyne's sermons were always based on Scripture and addressed major biblical themes such as "the rebellion and the fall of man, salvation by grace, the love of Christ and the wretchedness of the godless. The unbelievers in particular received much attention."[9] Even in the first year of his pastoral ministry, he was sensitive to season themes such as judgment and eternal punishment with genuine compassion for his hearers. On one occasion, he asked his friend Andrew Bonar what subject he had preached upon that week. Bonar replied that his subject had been, "The wicked shall be turned into hell." On hearing this, M'Cheyne asked his friend, "Were you able to preach it *with tenderness*?"[10] M'Cheyne's diary entry of June 15, 1836, reflects a similar concern: "Large meeting in the evening. Felt very *happy* after it,

---

7. A. Bonar, *Memoir and Remains*, 39.

8. A. Bonar, *Memoir and Remains*, 39–40.

9. Leen J. Van Valen, *Constrained by His Love: A New Biography on Robert Murray McCheyne*, trans. Laurence R. Noculson (Geanies House, Scotland: Christian Focus, 2002), 121.

10. A. Bonar, *Memoir and Remains*, 43.

though mourning for *bitter speaking of the gospel*. Surely it is a gentle message and should be spoken with angelic tenderness, especially by such a needy sinner."[11]

Another quality seen early in M'Cheyne's preaching ministry was his desire that Christ alone receive the glory through his messages. He wrote in his diary, "June 22.—Carron-shore. My last. Some tears; yet I fear some like the messenger, not the message; and I fear I am so vain as to love that love. Lord, let it not be so. Perish my honour, but let thine be exalted for ever."[12] On July 8, he wrote, *"I see a man cannot be a faithful minister, until he preaches Christ for Christ's sake*—until he gives up striving to attract people to himself, and seeks only to attract them to Christ. Lord, give me this!"[13]

Whether preaching or visiting in homes, M'Cheyne was always motivated by a desire to reach the lost. One Sunday evening, he was returning home after a tiring day of ministry. Someone brought to his attention that there were two families of gypsies staying nearby. Weary, yet desirous of reaching them, M'Cheyne set off to find them. Andrew Bonar writes, "By the side of their wood-fire he opened out the parable of the Lost Sheep, and pressed it on their souls in simple terms. He then knelt down in prayer for them and left them somewhat impressed, and very grateful."[14]

M'Cheyne spent just one year as an assistant to John Bonar in Larbert and Dunipace before accepting a call to St. Peter's Church in Dundee. The notes of his farewell sermon, preached in both Larbert and Dunipace, have been preserved for us. His farewell message, which was strongly evangelistic, was based on Jeremiah 8:20–22. Its title, based on verse 20, is "The Harvest Is Past, the Summer Is Ended." He had in mind those people who had heard his preaching but had not yet come to faith. Beginning with his text from Jeremiah, he stressed the urgency of the need for his

---

11. A. Bonar, *Memoir and Remains*, 43.
12. A. Bonar, *Memoir and Remains*, 44.
13. A. Bonar, *Memoir and Remains*, 45 (italics in the original).
14. A. Bonar, *Memoir and Remains*, 47.

hearers to put their faith in Jesus Christ as Savior. These are some of his concluding words from that message:

> But when there is a balm in Gilead and a Good Physician there; when Christ is a covert from the storm and the shadow of a great rock in this weary land; when the crucified Jesus is a ladder from earth to heaven; when there the veil has been rent from the top to the bottom; when there is a fountain in Jesus' blood to which the guiltiest may go; when there is a Saviour given as a ransom for all; when the Lord Jesus hath bid us this day declare that He does not wish the vilest, the sleepiest, the most vicious of you all to perish, Ah! How can we leave you thus unconverted, thus unawakened?[15]

His farewell message to the people of Larbert and Dunipace illustrates the great passion of the young pastor's heart—that his hearers would know the Savior whom he so dearly loved.

His Call to Dundee

In a letter to his parents on June 30, 1836, M'Cheyne wrote of the possibility of being called to Dundee. A church had been built there to serve a new parish that had been carved out of the crowded city, and a pastor was needed. He was to be considered for the position, and so were his good friends Alexander Somerville and Andrew Bonar. Concerning this, he wrote in the June letter to his parents, "I have no doubt we will contend with all humility, in honour preferring one another. If the people have any sense, they will choose Andrew Bonar, who, for learning, experimental knowledge, and all the valuable qualities of a minister, outshines all the students I ever knew."[16]

Despite his humble assessment of the choice before the people, M'Cheyne was called as the pastor to St. Peter's Church in Dundee. He was ordained at St. Peter's on November 24, 1836. On the

15. Robert Murray M'Cheyne, *Old Testament Sermons*, ed. Michael D. McMullen (Edinburgh: Banner of Truth, 2004), 112.

16. Smellie, *Robert Murray M'Cheyne*, 53.

following Sunday, he preached his first sermon as minister there on Isaiah 61:1–3, "The Spirit of the Lord God is upon Me...." He wrote of that text, "May it be prophetic of the object of my coming here!"[17] The choice of this passage indicates M'Cheyne's strong awareness that his ministry would only be effective if empowered by the Holy Spirit. He returned to preach from the same text each year on the anniversary of his ordination.

From the start, his ministry at St. Peter's was blessed with evidence of the Spirit's work. M'Cheyne later learned that two hearers had come to faith during his first sermon. St. Peter's was a large church, seating about 1,100 people, and it was crowded from the beginning. People even stood in hallways and sat on the pulpit steps to hear the young pastor, and the sense of God's presence as he preached was evident to many. James Hamilton wrote to Andrew Bonar of "the Bethel-like sacredness of Sabbaths and Communions" and of "the peculiar impression of 'God is here.'"[18]

In addition to preaching on Sunday mornings and afternoons, M'Cheyne began a Thursday night prayer meeting. This was something new in the religious customs of Dundee, but as many as 800 people came.[19] As on Sundays, God's presence was known in these meetings. M'Cheyne wrote of the Thursday services: "they will be remembered in Eternity with songs of praise."[20]

M'Cheyne especially focused on the spiritual growth of the children in Dundee. He began a weekly evening class using the Bible and the catechism as his textbooks. He gave special care to preparing God-fearing young people to take the Lord's Supper. Andrew Bonar notes that M'Cheyne's tract, *This Do in Remembrance of Me*, contains the substance of his teaching on these occasions.[21] The tract, published in 1840, contains detailed teaching on the Lord's Supper and concludes with a series of questions to young communicants.

---

17. A. Bonar, *Memoir and Remains*, 54.
18. Smellie, *Robert Murray M'Cheyne*, 58.
19. Smellie, *Robert Murray M'Cheyne*, 62.
20. Smellie, *Robert Murray M'Cheyne*, 62.
21. A. Bonar, *Memoir and Remains*, 61.

Some of those questions are:

1. Is it to please your father or mother, or any one on earth, that you think of coming to the Lord's table?

9. Do you think you have been awakened by the Holy Spirit? brought to Christ? born again? What makes you think so?

10. What is the meaning of the broken bread and poured-out wine?[22]

M'Cheyne clearly believed in the great value of ministry to children in the areas of both evangelism and discipleship. In his farewell sermon at Larbert and Dunipace, which he preached again at St. Peter's, he emphasized his belief that the best time to be converted is during one's youth, stating, "The heart is the tenderest in youth." He explained that during youth, a person's heart is not yet enslaved by "the cold and creeping selfishness of money-making manhood."[23]

In addition to his tract on the Lord's Supper for young communicants, he wrote other tracts specifically to communicate the gospel to children and to urge them to follow Christ. Others include *Reasons Why Children Should Fly to Christ* and *To the Lambs of the Flock*.[24]

M'Cheyne held high standards for those who would be allowed to teach children. To a woman interested in teaching a class for girls, he wrote that "she should be a Christian woman, not in name only, but in deed and truth,—one whose heart has been touched by the Spirit of God, and who can love the souls of little children. Any teacher who wanted this last qualification, I would look upon as a curse rather than a blessing."[25]

In addition to maintaining his ministries of preaching and discipleship, M'Cheyne continued his practice of home visitation in

22. A. Bonar, *Memoir and Remains*, 576.
23. M'Cheyne, *Old Testament Sermons*, 104–5.
24. Both are contained in the *Memoir and Remains of Robert Murray M'Cheyne*.
25. A. Bonar, *Memoir and Remains*, 62.

Dundee, and his visits were not limited to the members of St. Peter's Church. The parish of St. Peter's was made up of four thousand people, many of whom never attended any church, yet M'Cheyne longed to reach them. His tireless labor certainly may have contributed to his continuing struggles with physical health. Andrew Bonar writes concerning his friend, "Many of us thought that he afterward erred in the abundant frequency of his evangelistic labours at a time when he was still bound to a particular flock."[26] While M'Cheyne felt compelled by the love of Christ to pour himself out in evangelistic pastoral visitation, his zeal for evangelism is most clearly seen in his preaching.

---

26. A. Bonar, *Memoir and Remains*, 60.

Chapter 3

❧

Preaching, Theology,
and Pastoral Letters

The sermons of Robert Murray M'Cheyne reveal a remarkable depth of spiritual maturity, especially for one who began his pastorate at St. Peter's Church when he was only twenty-three years old. His preaching also indicates his extensive knowledge of the Bible. M'Cheyne preached freely from both the Old and New Testaments, and his topics, while always biblical, varied widely.

He once preached a message at St. Peter's from Numbers 22:32 (the story of Balaam's donkey) on the subject of "God's Care for the Animal Creation."[1] He spoke often of the terror of future judgment for the unconverted in messages like "God's Rectitude in Future Judgment" and "Future Punishment Eternal," but he also frequently told of God's compassion and love in sermons like "The Saviour's Tears Over the Lost," "The Love of Christ," and "Christ's Love to the Church."[2] M'Cheyne's preaching was focused on themes such as the holiness of God, the sinfulness of humanity, the atonement of Christ, and the gift of the righteousness of Christ to believers. Iain Murray writes, "Ruin by the fall,

---

1. Robert Murray M'Cheyne, *Old Testament Sermons*, ed. Michael D. McMullen (Edinburgh: Banner of Truth, 2004), 1–8.

2. Robert Murray M'Cheyne, *Sermons of Robert Murray M'Cheyne* (1961; repr., Edinburgh: Banner of Truth, 2000).

righteousness by Christ, and regeneration by the Spirit was the subject of his preaching."[3]

Regardless of his text, M'Cheyne focused on two key goals in his preaching: (1) present the gospel and urge the unconverted to faith in Christ, and (2) urge believers toward a life of holiness and devotion to Jesus. One of his earliest sermons, "The Love of Christ," based on 2 Corinthians 5:14, reveals these twin emphases. M'Cheyne first sets the verse in its context and then applies it to the lives of his hearers. Addressing unbelievers, he says: "Is there any of you, then, brethren, desirous of being made new—of being delivered from the slavery of sinful habits and affections? We can point you to no other remedy than the love of Christ.... Under a sense of your sins, flee to the Saviour of sinners."[4] Addressing believers, he continues: "We are constrained to holiness by the love of Christ; the love of him who loved us, is the only cord by which we are bound to the service of God.... Whosoever, then, would live a life of persevering holiness, let him keep his eye fixed on the Saviour."[5]

The same two emphases can be seen in one of M'Cheyne's sermons with a very different theme. His message, "Future Punishment Eternal," was based on Mark 9:44: "Where their worm dieth not, and the fire is not quenched." Here, M'Cheyne is very persuasive in urging ministers to speak more of hell, asserting that "they that have most love in their hearts speak most of hell."[6] He draws this message to a close by addressing believers: "Dear brothers and sisters, all this hell that I have described is what you and I deserved. We were over the lake of fire, but it was from this that Jesus saved us.... He drank every drop out of the cup of God's wrath for you and me—he died the just for the unjust. O! beloved,

---

3. Iain H. Murray, "Robert Murray M'Cheyne: Minister of St. Peter's, Dundee, 1836–1843," *Banner of Truth*, November 12, 2001, http://banneroftruth.org/us/resources/articles/2001/robert-murray-mcheyne/.

4. M'Cheyne, *Sermons of Robert Murray M'Cheyne*, 8.

5. M'Cheyne, *Sermons of Robert Murray M'Cheyne*, 11–12.

6. M'Cheyne, *Sermons of Robert Murray M'Cheyne*, 166.

how we should prize, love, and adore Jesus for what he has done for us."[7] Addressing the unbelievers in his audience he continues, "O! if it be true—if there be a furnace of fire—if there be a second death—if it is not an annihilation, but an eternal hell—O! is it reasonable to go on living in sin?… The bitterest thought will be, that you heard about hell, and yet rejected Christ. O! then, turn ye, turn ye, why will ye die?"[8]

We might think that one who spoke so freely about sin and eternal punishment would sound judgmental in his preaching. But in M'Cheyne, the uncompromising proclamation of God's Word was joined with an unusual sense of grace and compassion. His sermon notes from a message delivered on November 22, 1835, include these words: "I desire to speak with all reverence and with all tenderness upon so dreadful a subject. The man who speaks of hell should do it with tears in his eyes."[9]

Van Valen writes that M'Cheyne's "greatest gift lay, not in the manner of his delivery, but in the simplicity with which he rendered the good news of salvation. St. Peter's pulpit was filled with breath of the power of God's Spirit. Everyone felt that Christ's messenger had come into their midst, a man who was filled with compassion for lost souls."[10] In *Old Time Revivals*, John Shearer writes, "But M'Cheyne was himself his greatest sermon, and here is the secret of his success. He walked with God in the beauty of holiness. Our Lord's presence seemed to envelop him, diffusing a heavenly aroma. His very manner, his bearing as if a man standing in God's presence, was often the means of awakening indifferent sinners, so that men who could not remember a word he said

7. M'Cheyne, *Sermons of Robert Murray M'Cheyne*, 172–73.

8. M'Cheyne, *Sermons of Robert Murray M'Cheyne*, 173.

9. Robert Murray M'Cheyne, *From the Preacher's Heart* (1846; repr., Geanies House, Scotland: Christian Focus, 1993), 35.

10. Leen J. Van Valen, *Constrained by His Love: A New Biography on Robert Murray McCheyne*, trans. Laurence R. Noculson (Geanies House, Scotland: Christian Focus, 2002), 150.

found themselves with an unforgettable impression that God had drawn very near to them."[11]

His Theology

M'Cheyne's effectiveness as a preacher was built upon a strong foundation of theological understanding. According to David Haslam, "M'Cheyne read widely, and found great instruction and help from some of the great writers of the past, including Martin Luther, Jonathan Edwards, Richard Baxter, John Bunyan, to name but four."[12] Haslam goes on to describe M'Cheyne's theology as:

> An experiential Calvinism, just another term for a truly Biblical Christianity. His preaching was rooted and grounded in the Word of God, and took for its great themes the doctrines of the Westminster Confession of Faith and the Westminster Catechisms, the historic standards of Presbyterianism. The theology that united M'Cheyne and his companions was both Calvinistic and experiential. There was no false division between theory and practice in their lives.[13]

M'Cheyne held strongly to his understanding of God's sovereignty in the salvation of humans. Yet he also stressed the offer of the gospel to all people and man's responsibility to respond in faith to that offer, as is illustrated in his sermon "Electing Love." His message was based on John 15:16, "You did not choose Me, but I chose you and appointed you that you should go and bear fruit, and that your fruit should remain." M'Cheyne makes the point that "the natural ear is so deaf that it cannot hear; the natural eye is so blind that it cannot see Christ. It is true in one sense, that every disciple chooses Christ; but it is when God opens the eye to see him—it is when God gives strength to the withered arm to

---

11. John Shearer, *Old Time Revivals* (Philadelphia: Million Testaments Campaign, 1932), 66.

12. David F. Haslam, "Robert Murray M'Cheyne (1813–1843)" (from August 13, 2003 lecture), www.mcheyne.info/rmm.pdf, 1.

13. Haslam, "Robert Murray M'Cheyne (1813–1843)," 1.

embrace him."[14] M'Cheyne goes on to speak of why God chooses some: "the only reason given in the Bible why Christ loved us— and if you study till you die you will not find another—is, 'I will have mercy on whom I will have mercy.'"[15] Then, stressing both the initiative of God and the responsibility of man, M'Cheyne says, "Salvation is like a golden chain let down from heaven to earth; two links are in the hand of God—election and final salvation; but some of the links are on earth—conversion, adoption, etc."[16] He moves to close the message with these words, "Whether you are elected or not, I know not, but this I know—if you believe on Christ you will be saved."[17]

In another message, one based on Proverbs 8:4, M'Cheyne set forth the doctrine that "Christ offers Himself as a Saviour to all of the human race."[18] He goes on to explain, "Nobody ever came to Christ because they knew themselves to be of the elect. It is quite true that God has of His mere good pleasure elected some to everlasting life, but they never knew it till they came to Christ. Christ nowhere invites the elect to come to Him. The question for you is not, Am I one of the elect? but, Am I of the human race?"[19]

His Pastoral Letters

M'Cheyne continued to suffer physical illness throughout his pastorate at St. Peter's. After two years of service at Dundee, he began experiencing heart palpitations, and his medical advisors recommended that he withdraw from ministry for a season of complete rest. He returned to the home of his parents in Edinburgh for recuperation, hoping it would only be for a week or two. But it was months rather than weeks that he was away from his flock.

14. M'Cheyne, *Sermons of Robert Murray M'Cheyne*, 138–39.

15. M'Cheyne, *Sermons of Robert Murray M'Cheyne*, 141.

16. M'Cheyne, *Sermons of Robert Murray M'Cheyne*, 142.

17. M'Cheyne, *Sermons of Robert Murray M'Cheyne*, 143.

18. Andrew A. Bonar, *Memoir and Remains of Robert Murray M'Cheyne* (1844; repr., Edinburgh: Banner of Truth Trust, 2004), 366.

19. A. Bonar, *Memoir and Remains*, 369.

The young pastor grieved his absence from the people at Dundee, whom he had come to love. But his absence became the occasion for ministry to his church through letters. Beginning in January 1839, M'Cheyne wrote ten pastoral letters to St. Peter's Church. His letters tell us much about his compassionate heart for his members and his zeal for the Spirit's work in their lives.

M'Cheyne's pastoral letters contain several key themes. One of these was the urgent need for the unconverted to turn in faith to Jesus Christ for salvation. His letters were addressed to the church at large, and M'Cheyne was aware there were some at St. Peter's who were not yet believers. His first letter contains encouragement for those who were already Christians, as well as an exhortation for those who were not. Part of that letter reads,

> Be entreated, O wavering souls, to settle the question of your salvation now. Why halt ye between two opinions? It is most unreasonable to be undecided about the things of an endless eternity in such a world as this, with such frail bodies, with such a Saviour stretching out the hands, and such a Spirit of love striving with you. Remember you are flesh. You will soon hear your last sermon.[20]

He also addressed the theme of prayer in his letters. M'Cheyne knew some of the elders of his church were gathering on Monday evenings to pray for his recovery and for the church, and he assured the church he was praying for them as well. In his second letter, dated February 6, 1839, M'Cheyne writes, "Still He allowed me to give myself unto prayer. Perhaps this may be the chief reason of my exile from you, to teach me what Zechariah was taught in the vision of the golden candlestick and the two olive trees (Zech. 4): that it is not by might nor by power, but by His Spirit obtained in believing, wrestling prayer that the temple of God is to be built in our parishes."[21]

---

20. Robert Murray M'Cheyne, *Pastoral Letters* (1844; repr., Shoals, Ind.: Kingsley, 2003), 17.

21. M'Cheyne, *Pastoral Letters*, 23.

His letter of February 20, 1839, is essentially a teaching on prayer and is filled with instruction and encouragement to pray:

> Christ never loses one believing prayer. The prayers of every believer—from Abel to the present day—He heaps upon the altar from which they are continually ascending before His Father and our Father; and when the altar can hold no more, the full answer will come down. Do not be discouraged, dearly beloved, because God bears long with you—because He does not seem to answer your prayers. When the merchant sends his ships to distant shores, he does not expect them to come back richly laden in a single day. He has great patience…. Perhaps your prayers will come back like the ships of the merchant—all the more heavily laden with blessings because of the delay.[22]

His closing paragraph of this letter reads, "These things I have written that you may have greater confidence in coming to the throne of grace. The Lord make you a praying people."[23]

Another theme in M'Cheyne's pastoral letters is the need for growth in holiness and devotion to Christ. M'Cheyne believed it was necessary for Christians to continue to grow spiritually throughout life. He wrote, "The only way to be kept from falling is 'to grow.' If you stand still, you will fall."[24] As always, he pointed his church to God Himself as the source of their growth, and his letter of March 13, 1839, includes these words: "Seek to be made holier every day. Pray, strive, wrestle for the Spirit to make you like God. Be as much as you can with God. I declare to you that I had rather be one hour with God than a thousand with the sweetest society on earth or in heaven. All other joys are but streams—God is the fountain."[25]

As the faithful pastor recovered at his parents' home in Edinburgh, he also wrote to his church on the topic of suffering.

---

22. M'Cheyne, *Pastoral Letters*, 40–41.

23. M'Cheyne, *Pastoral Letters*, 43.

24. M'Cheyne, *Pastoral Letters*, 66.

25. M'Cheyne, *Pastoral Letters*, 66.

His letter of February 13, 1839, includes a short teaching on Job 23:8–10. Here, Job states his belief that, though he cannot see the Lord, "when He has tested me, I shall come forth as gold" (v. 10). M'Cheyne used this text to encourage his members who were suffering affliction, reminding them that God is closer than even the closest friend in our times of suffering: "Still be of good cheer, the Father of all the best of friends knows well the way you take."[26] He assured them suffering always has an end for the Christian, writing, "This also is precious comfort. There will be an end of your affliction. Christians must have 'great tribulation,' but they come out of it. We must carry the cross—but only for a moment—then comes the crown."[27]

Finally he wrote to them of the purifying effect of affliction in a believer's life. He continues, "But shall we come out the same as we went in? Oh no! 'We shall come out like gold.' It is this that sweetens the bitterest cup. This brings a rainbow of promise over the darkest cloud. Affliction will *certainly* purify a believer."[28]

M'Cheyne drew this letter to a close with a request for the prayers of his members: "Finally, pray that your pastor may come out of his trials like gold."[29] This is one of only a few times when M'Cheyne spoke of his own physical suffering during his absence from his church. His attention was clearly focused on the spiritual health of his church rather than his own physical well-being.

While M'Cheyne would never fully recover from his own physical ailments, his ministry would continue to take shape despite his afflictions. In fact, his suffering would have a part in his decision to pursue a ministry trip to another land.

---

26. M'Cheyne, *Pastoral Letters*, 33.
27. M'Cheyne, *Pastoral Letters*, 33.
28. M'Cheyne, *Pastoral Letters*, 34.
29. M'Cheyne, *Pastoral Letters*, 35.

Chapter 4

—————— ❧ ——————

The Mission of Discovery

M'Cheyne felt a call to world missions soon after his conversion, as can be seen from an entry he made in his diary on November 12, 1831. He had been reading *The Life and Letters of Henry Martyn* and was moved by the sacrificial commitment of this missionary to India and Persia.[1] His diary records, "Reading H. Martyn's Memoirs. Would I could imitate him, giving up father, mother, country, house, health, life, all—for Christ. And yet, what hinders? Lord, purify me, and give me strength to dedicate myself, my all to Thee!"[2] Several months later, M'Cheyne had apparently been reading *Life of David Brainerd*, by Jonathan Edwards.[3] After reading of this young missionary to the American Indians, he wrote, "June 27.—Life of David Brainerd. Most wonderful man! What conflicts, what depressions, desertions, strength, advancement, victories, within thy torn bosom! I cannot express what I think when I think of thee. To-night, more set upon missionary enterprise than ever."[4]

His interest in missions was combined with a particular interest in ministry to the Jewish people. Andrew Bonar records that

1. John Sargent, *The Life and Letters of Henry Martyn* (Edinburgh: Banner of Truth, 1985).

2. Andrew A. Bonar, *Memoir and Remains of Robert Murray M'Cheyne* (1844; repr., Edinburgh: Banner of Truth, 2004), 13.

3. Jonathan Edwards and Norman Pettit, *The Life of David Brainerd* (New Haven: Yale University Press, 1985).

4. A. Bonar, *Memoir and Remains*, 18.

M'Cheyne often made the point that "we should be like God in His particular affections; and the whole Bible shows that God has ever had, and still has, a peculiar love to the Jews."[5] A letter written by M'Cheyne expresses his belief that missions efforts toward Jews could result in revival in the Church of Scotland: "To seek the lost sheep of the house of Israel is an object very near to my heart, as my people know it has ever been. Such an enterprise may probably draw down unspeakable blessings on the Church of Scotland, according to the promise, 'They shall prosper who love Thee.'"[6]

While still recovering from illness at his parents' home in Edinburgh, M'Cheyne received an invitation which appealed both to his interest in missions and in ministry to the Jewish people. The General Assembly of the Church of Scotland had appointed two men, Dr. Alexander Keith and Dr. Alexander Black, to explore opportunities for a mission to the Jews in Central Europe or Asia Minor. It had been suggested that M'Cheyne and Andrew Bonar be part of the exploratory team. M'Cheyne was immediately interested but sought the advice of his medical caregivers about how such a trip might affect his health. Surprisingly, his medical friends felt the travel might actually be good for him.

The members of St. Peter's Church, however, were not so enthusiastic about their pastor undertaking the trip and extending his leave from them. When he learned of their concern, M'Cheyne sought to put them at ease by writing, "God has very plainly shown me that I may perform a deeply important work for His ancient people, and at the same time be in the best way of seeking a return of health."[7] Being thus assured, the people of St. Peter's sent their pastor a letter granting their blessing. Their letter reveals both the love they had for their pastor and the vision they shared for his success in God's work:

5. A. Bonar, *Memoir and Remains*, 88.

6. A. Bonar, *Memoir and Remains*, 87.

7. A. Bonar, *Memoir and Remains*, 88.

May God be the Companion of your journey. May He refresh your soul by rich communications of His love. May He conduct you in safety to the place of your destination. And when your feet stand amidst the ruins of the once-glorious Temple, on that Mount Zion which was *beautiful for situation, the joy of the whole earth*, may the Spirit Himself come down upon you *as the dew of Hermon, the dew that descended upon the mountains of Zion.*[8]

Having arranged for William C. Burns to serve in an interim pastoral role at St. Peter's, M'Cheyne began making arrangements for the trip. The Mission of Inquiry, as it came to be called, would also help prepare the way for future missionary efforts from the Church of Scotland. So significant was the mission to M'Cheyne's life that historian Marcus Loane writes, "His full career as a preacher was to divide into two three-year terms, with his journey to the Holy Land in between."[9]

M'Cheyne, Bonar, Keith, and Black left Scotland for London in the spring of 1839. On arrival there, they secured their passports and "letters to her Majesty's foreign consuls."[10] They were also supplied with a variety of gospel tracts in different languages by the Religious Tract Society.

They sailed from Dover on the morning of April 12, 1839. M'Cheyne and Andrew Bonar kept remarkably detailed notes about the Mission of Inquiry and their travels, which would later be published as the *Narrative of a Mission of Inquiry to the Jews from the Church of Scotland in 1839*. By 1847, twenty-three thousand copies of the *Narrative* were in print, and it would be significantly used by God to help motivate Christians in Scotland to support

---

8. Alexander Smellie, *Robert Murray M'Cheyne* (1913; repr., Geanies House, Scotland: Christian Focus, 1995), 82–83.

9. Marcus L. Loane, *They Were Pilgrims* (Edinburgh: Banner of Truth, 2006), 149.

10. Andrew Bonar and R. M. McCheyne, *Mission of Discovery: The Beginnings of Modern Jewish Evangelism*, originally published as *Narrative of a Mission of Inquiry to the Jews from the Church of Scotland in 1839*, ed. Allan M. Harman, (1839; repr., Geanies House, Scotland: Christian Focus, 1966), 19.

Jewish missions.[11] The detailed *Narrative* (over 400 pages in currently published copies) provides insight into the spiritual beliefs and practices of Jews in 1839. But it also tells us much about the difficulties of travel in that day and the remarkable challenges faced by missionaries.

Leaving London, the group traveled through France, Italy, Greece, and Egypt. Desert travel was particularly difficult as noted in their journal entry of March 25:

> The sunbeams glanced along the level plain of the wilderness, scorching our hands and faces, for we were journeying nearly due east. Every hour it became hotter and hotter, and this, along with the slow rocking motion of the camel, often produced irresistible drowsiness—a feeling indescribably painful in such circumstances. About half-past nine o'clock, a loud cry from the guide aroused us all. Our friend Dr. Black had fallen suddenly from his camel. We immediately slipped down from our camels and ran to the spot. For some time he remained nearly insensible, but by the use of such restoratives as we had, at last began gradually to recover. It was a truly affecting scene, which we can never forget. Far from our kindred, in the midst of a vast solitude, no living being near except our little company of Arabs, not knowing what might be the extent of the injury received, we felt how completely our times were in God's hand.[12]

A May 30 entry reads:

> The heat was very oppressive. Even the Bedouins begged us to lend them handkerchiefs to shield their faces from the rays of the sun; and often ran before and threw themselves beneath a bush to find shelter for a few minutes. How full of meaning did the word of the prophet appear, "There shall be a tabernacle for a shadow in the daytime from the heat"

---

11. Bonar and McCheyne, *Mission of Discovery*, 17.
12. Bonar and McCheyne, *Mission of Discovery*, 75.

(Isaiah 4:6). And again, "A man shall be as the shadow of a great rock in a weary land" (Isaiah 32:2).[13]

One of the most remarkable things about the *Narrative* is the abundant use of Scripture to link locations to biblical history. An example is seen in their notes of June 4 after observing the town of Gaza:

> Whilst we gazed upon this peaceful scene, we felt it hard to think that this was a land on which God was "laying his vengeance" (Ezekiel 25:17). It appeared at first as if there had been no fulfillment of those distinct predictions, "Gaza shall be forsaken" (Zephaniah 2:4), and "baldness has come upon Gaza" (Jeremiah 47:5). But when we had completed our investigations, we found that not one word had fallen to the ground.[14]

Their description of an area on June 6 includes these words:

> The situation and name of these villages at once suggested to us that this is the valley of Zephathah where Asa defeated Zerah, the Ethiopian, with his host of "a thousand thousand" (2 Chronicles 14:9). In this vast plain there would be room enough for all that multitude, and ample scope in these level fields for the three hundred chariots. We remembered with fresh interest also, how the ark of God was carried by the two milch kine from the land of the Philistines to Beth-Shemesh, across this very plain, probably a little north of us (2 Samuel 6:12). Nor could we lift our eyes to the hill country of Judah without remembering the visit of the mother of our Lord to her cousin Elizabeth (Luke 1:39). Once also Mareshah, Lachish and Libnah stood in this vast plain.[15]

Despite the demands of travel and the need for detailed notes of their trip, M'Cheyne still found time to write letters to family and friends, to compose poetry, and even to draw illustrations of

---

13. Bonar and McCheyne, *Mission of Discovery*, 81.
14. Bonar and McCheyne, *Mission of Discovery*, 93.
15. Bonar and McCheyne, *Mission of Discovery*, 100.

places they visited. His detailed letter to the Rev. R. MacDonald of Blairgowrie was written on June 26 from Mount Carmel to share with his friend what he was learning about Israel. The lengthy letter includes these words:

> The first sight of Jerusalem made my heart sink within me, it was so desolate, the walls appeared so low, so dark, so poor. But better acquaintance with its deep valleys and singular hills, its trees and fountains, has made it appear one of the loveliest spots Jesus visited. There is a holy beauty about Jerusalem; for you cannot walk a step without remembering the scenes that have passed there, and without looking forward to a time when it will again become the joy of the whole earth.[16]

His letter to MacDonald includes an emphasis found in many of his letters—encouragement toward a life of holiness. He writes, "Ah, dear friend, wherever we journey, union to Jesus, and holiness from His Spirit flowing into us, is our chief and only happiness. Never cease to show your people that to be holy is to be happy and that to bring us to perfect holiness and likeness to God, was the very end for which Christ died."[17]

The same letter notes that one of M'Cheyne's favorite spots to visit had been the fountain of Siloam. He promised his friend, "I send you a small hymn on the other side, which will imprint it on your memory."[18] This hymn is apparently his own poem, entitled "Fountain of Siloam." Its words reveal M'Cheyne's ever-present longing to tell others about His Savior.

> Beneath Moriah's rocky side
> A gentle fountain springs;
> Silent and soft its waters glide,
> Like the peace the Spirit brings.
>
> The thirsty Arab stoops to drink
> Of the cool and quiet wave;

---

16. A. Bonar, *Memoir and Remains*, 269.
17. A. Bonar, *Memoir and Remains*, 269.
18. A. Bonar, *Memoir and Remains*, 271.

> And the thirsty spirit stops to think
> Of Him who came to save.
>
> Siloam is the fountain's name,
> It means "One sent from God,"
> And thus the Holy Saviour's fame
> It gently spreads abroad.
>
> O grant that I, like this sweet well,
> May Jesus' image bear,
> And spend my life, my all, to tell
> How full His mercies are.
>
> Foot of Carmel, June 1839.[19]

M'Cheyne's letters and poems composed during the Mission of Inquiry reveal that the trip was about much more than fact-finding. This journey to the Holy Land was for him a time of sweet fellowship with the One who had walked this land when He lived on earth. The closing words from his poem "The Sea of Galilee" reveal his desire to increasingly know the depths of God's love.

> Oh! give me, Lord, by this sacred wave,
> Threefold Thy love divine,
> That I may feed, till I find my grave,
> Thy flock—both Thine and mine.[20]

The beautiful faith expressed by M'Cheyne in his letters and poems was often tested during the mission. At one point, M'Cheyne became so sick with a fever that he lost his memory for a short period, and he barely spoke for three days. A kind couple in the village of Bouja, in Smyrna, nursed him back to health. To friends at home, M'Cheyne wrote:

I left the foot of Lebanon when I could hardly see, or hear, or speak, or remember; I felt my faculties going, one by one, and I had every reason to expect that I would soon be with my

---

19. A. Bonar, *Memoir and Remains*, 640. M'Cheyne references Isaiah 8:6 for this poem.

20. A. Bonar, *Memoir and Remains*, 640–41.

God. It is a sore trial to be alone and dying in a foreign land, and it has made me feel, in a way that I never knew before, the necessity of having unfeigned faith in Jesus and in God.[21]

The group faced a number of life-threatening challenges on the trip. The fall from his camel and related health issues meant Dr. Black was unable to complete the trip. He and Dr. Keith returned home by another route. On one occasion, M'Cheyne could easily have been killed by robbers. Andrew Bonar explains that during their return through Poland, M'Cheyne and he had separated for a time of quiet meditation. M'Cheyne found a secluded spot but was soon approached by two Polish shepherds. A struggle ensued until M'Cheyne lay exhausted on the ground. Then the two men suddenly ran away. Bonar writes, "What moved them so suddenly to depart, we could not conjecture. We felt that the hand of God that had delivered us out of so many dangers during our previous wanderings had been eminently stretched out again."[22]

On their return home in November 1839, the travelers compiled a report for the General Assembly of the Church of Scotland. In 1840, the General Assembly resolved, *that the cause of Israel should from that time form one of the great missionary schemes of our church.*[23] Thus, the Mission of Inquiry would continue to bear fruit as Scottish missionaries sought to share the message of the Messiah with Jews for years to come. M'Cheyne must have surely rejoiced as he did when he wrote this poem, titled "On the Mediterranean Sea in the Bay of Carmel," during the Mission of Inquiry.

> O Lord, this swelling, tideless sea
> Is like Thy love in Christ to me:
> The ceaseless waves that fill the bay
> Through flinty rocks have worn their way,
> And Thy unceasing love alone
> Hath broken through this heart of stone.

21. A. Bonar, *Memoir and Remains*, 107.
22. Bonar and McCheyne, *Mission of Discovery*, 392.
23. Bonar and McCheyne, *Mission of Discovery*, 445.

The countless smile that gilds the deep
When sunbeams on the water sleep,
Is like Thy countless smile of grace
When I am seen in Jesus' face.

No ebbing tide these waters know,
Pure, placid, constant in their flow:
No ebb Thy love to me hath known
Since first it chose me for Thine own.
Or if, perchance, at Thy command,
The wave retiring leaves the sand,
One moment all is dry, and then
It turns to fill the shore again:
So I have found Thy wondrous grace
Forsake my soul a little space;
Barren and cold, deserted, dry,
A helpless worm to Thee I cry:
Thy face is hid a little while,
But with the morning comes Thy smile—
Jesus once more His beauty shows,
And all my heart with peace o'erflows.

These deep blue waters lave the shore
Of Israel, as in days of yore!
Though Zion like a field is ploughed,
And Salem's covered with a cloud—
Though briars and thorns are tangled o'er,
Where vine and olive twined before—
Though turbaned Moslems tread the gate,
And Judah sits most desolate—
Their nets o'er Tyre the fishers spread,
And Carmel's top is withered—
Yet still these waters clasp the shore
As kindly as they did before!
Such is Thy love to Judah's race,
A deep unchanging tide of grace.
Though scattered now at Thy command,

They pine away in every land,
With trembling heart and failing eyes,
And deep the veil on Israel lies,
Yet still Thy word Thou canst not break,
"Beloved for their father's sake."[24]

24. A. Bonar, *Memoir and Remains*, 643–44.

Chapter 5

—————— ❖•❖ ——————

Revival and M'Cheyne's Final Days

While Andrew Bonar and Robert Murray M'Cheyne were returning from the Holy Land, they began to hear reports of revival back in Scotland. W. C. Burns, who was filling M'Cheyne's pastorate in Dundee, had traveled to Kilsyth to preach in his father's church on July 23, 1839. While preaching that day and urging the receiving of Christ, the Holy Spirit had begun to work in a remarkable way. Many people sensed an urgent need to be in a right relationship with God.

W. C. Burns returned to St. Peter's to preach on August 8. On that day, M'Cheyne was suffering physically during the trip home; confined to bed, he was praying for his church at Dundee. As Burns brought the news of revival at Kilsyth to Dundee, the people were stirred. Two days later, during a prayer meeting, the Lord began working in Dundee as He had at Kilsyth.

M'Cheyne and Bonar actually read of the revival in a newspaper while sailing toward England. The article mentioned Dundee, so M'Cheyne was especially eager to hear more news. On arriving at his parents' home in Edinburgh, he wrote Burns to learn more. M'Cheyne's letter to Burns on November 15 reveals something of his remarkable humility in celebrating God's work through the interim pastor: "You remember it was the prayer of my heart when we parted, that you might be a thousandfold more blessed to the people than ever my ministry had been.

How it will gladden my heart, if you can really tell me that it has been so!"[1]

On returning to Dundee, M'Cheyne got more details of the remarkable awakening which had begun at St. Peter's during his absence. Andrew Bonar provides this record of what had taken place in Dundee after Burns returned from Kilsyth:

> On Thursday, the second day after his return, at the close of the usual evening prayer-meetings in St. Peter's, and when the minds of many were deeply solemnised by the tidings which had reached them, he spoke a few words about what had for some days detained him from them, and invited those to remain who felt the need of an outpouring of the Spirit to convert them. About a hundred remained; and at the conclusion of a solemn address to these anxious souls, suddenly the power of God seemed to descend, and all were bathed in tears. At a similar meeting next evening, in the church, there was much melting of heart and intense desire after the Beloved of the Father; and on adjourning to the vestry, the arm of the Lord was revealed. No sooner was the vestry-door opened to admit those who might feel anxious to converse, than a vast number pressed in with awful eagerness. It was like a pent-up flood breaking forth; tears were streaming from the eyes of many, and some fell on the ground groaning, and weeping, and crying for mercy. Onward from that evening, meetings were held every day for many weeks; and the extraordinary nature of the work justified and called for extraordinary services. The whole town was moved. Many believers doubted; the ungodly raged; but the Word of God grew mightily and prevailed.[2]

With such an extraordinary working of the Holy Spirit during his absence, M'Cheyne may have wondered whether his church would be happy to have him return. But the people were thrilled

---

1. Andrew A. Bonar, *Memoir and Remains of Robert Murray M'Cheyne* (1844; repr., Edinburgh: Banner of Truth, 2004), 273.

2. A. Bonar, *Memoir and Remains*, 114.

to see their pastor again, having prayed for him throughout his travels. He returned on a Thursday, and the church was filled to capacity that night when M'Cheyne preached. On Friday night, W. C. Burns delivered the message. Then on Sunday, M'Cheyne preached during one morning service while Burns preached the other, as well as the evening service. Here we see M'Cheyne's wisdom in continuing to share the pulpit with Burns. He avoided an abrupt transition during a time of such extraordinary evidence of the Lord's work.

Remarkably, there seems to have been no jealousy whatsoever between M'Cheyne and Burns. Further, there is no indication that the people of St. Peter's were divided in their loyalty to either man. Perhaps their lack of factiousness was a reflection of the humility shown by their pastor himself. Andrew Bonar writes of M'Cheyne's attitude during this time: "But Mr. M'Cheyne had received from the Lord a holy disinterestedness that suppressed every feeling of envy. Many wondered at the single-heartedness he was able to exhibit. He could sincerely say, 'I have no desire but the salvation of my people, by whatever instrument.'"[3]

M'Cheyne soon resumed fully his role as pastor at St. Peter's. The revival continued, but with some slowing by the end of the year. W. C. Burns continued to preach throughout Scotland, and the revival seen in Kilsyth and Dundee spread to other towns. In 1847, Burns would travel to the Far East to fulfill his dream of becoming a missionary.

Apparently, M'Cheyne had sufficient physical strength after the mission to continue visiting in homes and preaching regularly. He took special delight in quarterly Communion seasons when he would be joined by other ministers in serving the Lord's Supper to his flock. His diary notes of such a season in April 1840 indicate that revival was continuing in his parish. On Monday, April 20, he described the response in one service: "The sobbing soon spread, till many heads were bent down, and the church was filled with

---

3. A. Bonar, *Memoir and Remains*, 116.

sobbing. Many whom I did not know were now affected. After prayer, we dismissed near midnight. Many followed us. One, in great agony, prayed that she might find Christ that very night."[4]

While M'Cheyne continued his ministry to his flock, he also took joy in encouraging other ministers, becoming part of a ministerial prayer meeting in Dundee and meeting weekly to pray with others. He also continued to find time to encourage others toward holiness and humility by his letters. In a letter to W. C. Burns on November 3, 1841, he wrote: "Now remember Moses wist not that the skin of his face shone. Looking at our own shining face is the bane of the spiritual life and of the ministry. Oh for closest communion with God, till soul and body—head, face, and heart—shine with divine brilliancy! but oh, for a holy ignorance of our shining! Pray for this; for you need it as well as I."[5]

Another friend in ministry had written to M'Cheyne of the difficulty of the times and his discouragement with progress in his own church. M'Cheyne replied, "I am sure there was never a time when the Spirit of God was more present in Scotland, and it does not become you to murmur in your tents, but rather to give thanks. Remember, we may grieve the Spirit as truly by not joyfully acknowledging His wonders as by not praying for Him."[6]

The awakening that had occurred at St. Peter's was being experienced throughout Scotland. In 1840, the Presbytery of Aberdeen appointed a committee to research the revivals taking place in their churches. Because M'Cheyne was associated with revival, he was asked to respond to a number of questions from the committee. His response, completed on March 26, 1841, was later published as *Evidence on Revivals.*[7] The document affirms M'Cheyne's support of the revival and his belief that it was a genuine working of the Holy Spirit: "It is my decided and solemn conviction, in the sight of God, that a very remarkable and glorious work of God, in the

---

4. A. Bonar, *Memoir and Remains*, 128.
5. A. Bonar, *Memoir and Remains*, 130–31.
6. A. Bonar, *Memoir and Remains*, 131.
7. This is contained in A. Bonar, *Memoir and Remains*, 543–51.

conversion of sinners and edifying of saints, has taken place in this parish and neighbourhood."[8]

In his response, M'Cheyne expressed his belief that the most remarkable season of the revival had taken place while he was away on the Mission of Inquiry. Still, he had observed extraordinary things since his return. He wrote:

> Even since my return, however, I have myself frequently seen the preaching of the word attended with so much power, and eternal things brought so near, that the feelings of the people could not be restrained. I have observed at such times an awful and breathless stillness pervading the assembly; each hearer bent forward in the posture of rapt attention; serious men covered their faces to pray that the arrows of the King of Zion might be sent home with power to the hearts of sinners. Again, at such a time, I have heard a half-suppressed sigh rising from many a heart, and have seen many bathed in tears. At other times, I have heard loud sobbing in many parts of the Church, while a deep solemnity pervaded the whole audience. I have also, in some instances, heard individuals cry aloud, as if they had been pierced through with a dart. These solemn scenes were witnessed under the preaching of different ministers, and sometimes occurred under the most tender gospel invitations. On one occasion, for instance, when the minister was speaking tenderly on the words, "He is altogether lovely," almost every sentence was responded to by the cries of the bitterest agony. At such times I have seen persons so overcome, that they could not walk or stand alone. I have known cases in which believers have been similarly affected through the fullness of their joy.[9]

In response to the presbytery, M'Cheyne notes that he had studied revivals of the past, both in Scotland and around the world, to compare these with what had taken place in Dundee. He wrote: "In doing this, I have been fully convinced that the outpouring of

---

8. A. Bonar, *Memoir and Remains*, 544.
9. A. Bonar, *Memoir and Remains*, 547–48.

the Holy Spirit at the Kirk of Shotts, and again, a century after, at Cambuslang, etc., in Scotland, and under the ministry of President Edwards in America, was attended by the very same appearances as the work in our own day."[10]

M'Cheyne was persuaded that no unscriptural doctrines had been perpetrated during the revival. But he knew that another test of genuineness was the evidence of lasting fruit, and the many changed lives in his church and community provided that evidence. The story of one such changed life was shared by Rev. Thomas Alexander of London. Writing for the *Sabbath School Magazine* in 1860, he shares of his conversion during the revival at St. Peter's. At that time, he was ignorant of spiritual truth and given to frequent drunkenness. Someone urged him to go to St. Peter's to hear M'Cheyne preach. One snowy winter day, he made his way to the church for the afternoon service. In the church yard, he encountered a man he had known as a boy. The dramatic change in this man would speak mightily of the life-changing power of the gospel.

Rev. Alexander shares the story of the man in these words:

> As a boy I had known him; and he was the only man for whom I had a fear; but of him I had a thorough terror—I, and all the little boys of the village. He was a fierce, drunken, brutal savage; one of the sort that do actually kick and bite in their explosions of wrath. I had known him well. His features were, each of them, as familiar to me as were my own in the glass. There was no mistaking the man. That was he leaning there, with that sweet smile, and enjoying that pipe with so manifest an unction. I can never forget the effect of reading a chapter out of that living epistle; how every word I read there, in that man's quiet look, went to my heart. It was as if you had stood beside Saul of Tarsus on his way to Damascus, and heard the Lord Jesus speak to him from heaven. There it was—it is no shadow—the man stands looking curiously at you now; but that is he. "Are you _____?" The man quietly

---

10. A. Bonar, *Memoir and Remains*, 550.

nodded. "Yes, but I'm not the _____ you once knew." No, I could see that. Grace had changed the very face of the man. It had taken away his fierce look, and made him a man. So he told me his story: how he came here to curse, and remained to pray; and how he walked every Sabbath about seven miles to this church, and never thought the road long. I inquired, on my return home, what character the man now bore in his neighbourhood, and found that it was all that could be desired; his wife, in particular, though not herself converted, was nevertheless full of his praises now. Nothing so impressed me as that.[11]

Thomas Alexander then began attending St. Peter's Church and sitting under the preaching of M'Cheyne. He, too, would become a follower of Jesus and, eventually, a minister of the gospel.

One result of the revival which M'Cheyne and others may not have foreseen was its impact on evangelicalism in Scotland. For years, there had been growing tension between the moderates and evangelicals over the relationship of the church to civil authorities. The government provided significant support to the national church in Scotland and retained authority in the placement of ministers. Evangelicals believed that churches had a scriptural right to elect their own pastors, while the moderates submitted to the role of civil powers in that decision. The evangelicals had respected the parish boundaries of the moderates in the past, but things began to change with the revival. Zeal for evangelism compelled M'Cheyne and like-minded ministers to take the gospel to all people in Scotland. In the words of Iain Murray, "It was the revival in the Church of Scotland which led to the Disruption of that Church."[12]

The Disruption, as it came to be known, occurred on May 18, 1843, at a meeting of the General Assembly of the Church of Scotland. About one-third of the ministers, including Thomas

---

11. A. Bonar, *Memoir and Remains*, 200.
12. Iain H. Murray, *A Scottish Christian Heritage* (Edinburgh: Banner of Truth, 2006), 109.

Chalmers, broke away to form the Free Church of Scotland. This meant forsaking the financial support of the government, along with all church buildings, manses, and schools. The sacrifice of those who formed the Free Church of Scotland was significant. Had M'Cheyne still been alive, he would undoubtedly have been among them.

His Latter Days

M'Cheyne somehow knew that his time on earth would be brief. He once closed a sermon with these words, "Changes are coming; every eye before me shall soon be dim in death. Another pastor shall feed this flock; another singer lead the psalm; another flock fill this fold."[13] On another occasion, he wrote to a friend, "Use your health while you have it, my dear friend and brother. Do not cast away peculiar opportunities that may never come again. You know not when your last Sabbath with your people may come. Speak for eternity."[14]

It may have been M'Cheyne's belief that his life would be short that prevented him from ever marrying, although Alexander Smellie notes that he was twice engaged to be married in the last five or six years of his life.[15] While we cannot be sure of the reasons he never married, we can be sure of this—M'Cheyne lived with his thoughts and affections fixed on eternity. His sermons, letters, and diary all reveal a man who lived with an eternal perspective. This excerpt from a letter to a fellow minister shows the attitude that guided his life:

> May your mind be solemnised, my dear friend, by the thought that we are ministers but for a time; that the Master may summon us to retire into silence, or may call us to the temple above; or the midnight cry of the Bridegroom may break suddenly on our ears. Blessed is that servant that is

---

13. A. Bonar, *Memoir and Remains*, 159.

14. A. Bonar, *Memoir and Remains*, 93.

15. Alexander Smellie, *Robert Murray M'Cheyne* (1913; repr., Geanies House, Scotland: Christian Focus, 1995), 152.

found waiting! Make all your services tell for eternity; speak what you can look back upon with comfort when you must be silent.[16]

His desire to use all his strength in the service of his Master compelled M'Cheyne to continue to preach despite his illnesses. In the summer of 1842, he had several attacks of sickness, and he seemed to feel he was near death.[17] Yet he continued to preach, accepting a number of invitations beyond his own church.

During February 1843, M'Cheyne set out on what would be his last evangelistic tour. He spoke at twenty-four different places in three weeks. Andrew Bonar notes that M'Cheyne seemed to be exemplifying the words he was known to use: "The oil of the lamp in the temple burnt away in giving light; so should we."[18]

When M'Cheyne returned from the evangelistic meetings to his church on March 1, he was exhausted. Yet he continued preaching and ministering to the people of his parish. In his weakened state, he was exposed to typhus during home visitation.

On Sunday, March 12, 1843, he preached his very last sermon. That week he became seriously ill, with a fever so high it was difficult for him to even speak. But those who attended him occasionally heard him speak during his delirium—preaching or praying for his people. He was heard to say, "This parish, Lord, this people, this whole place!" "Do it Thyself, Lord, for Thy weak servant." "Holy Father, keep through Thine own Name those whom Thou has given me."[19]

On Saturday morning, March 25, 1843, a physician named Dr. Gibson was with M'Cheyne when he took his last breath. He lifted his hands as if pronouncing a blessing over his church, and his spirit left his body.[20]

16. A. Bonar, *Memoir and Remains*, 210.
17. A. Bonar, *Memoir and Remains*, 143.
18. A. Bonar, *Memoir and Remains*, 160.
19. A. Bonar, *Memoir and Remains*, 163–64.
20. A. Bonar, *Memoir and Remains*, 164.

His good friend Andrew Bonar was particularly struck by the news of M'Cheyne's death. Bonar's diary of March 25 reads: "This afternoon about 5 o'clock a message has just come to tell me of Robert M'Cheyne's death. Never, never in all my life have I felt anything like this. It is a blow to myself, to his people, to the Church of Christ in Scotland.... Life has lost half its joys, were it not for the hope of saving souls. There was no friend whom I have loved like him."[21]

The grief felt at St. Peter's, and throughout Dundee and all of Scotland, was likewise great. On the day of M'Cheyne's funeral, business was almost completely suspended throughout his parish.[22]

After M'Cheyne's death, a note was found unopened which had been addressed to him. It was from a person who had heard him speak on March 12, his last sermon. Part of the note reads: "I heard you preach last Sabbath evening, and it pleased God to bless that sermon to my soul. It was not so much what you said, as your manner of speaking that struck me. I saw in you a beauty of holiness that I never saw before."[23] The tribute to M'Cheyne written upon his death by Mr. Hamilton of London includes these words: "His public actings were a direct emanation from the most heavenly ingredient in his character—his love and gratitude to the Divine Redeemer."[24]

What was it about Robert Murray M'Cheyne that resulted in such love and gratitude to Jesus Christ? What brought such an evident sense of holiness to his life? Those are the questions we will now address as we consider M'Cheyne's all-surpassing fellowship— his communion with the living God.

---

21. Keith Walker, "Robert Murray M'Cheyne: Saint and Preacher," *The Banner of Truth*, no. 246 (March 1984, 18–26) http://web.ukonline.co.uk/d.haslam/mccheyne/kwalker1.htm, 7.

22. A. Bonar, *Memoir and Remains*, 170–71.

23. A. Bonar, *Memoir and Remains*, 161–62.

24. A. Bonar, *Memoir and Remains*, 172.

PART 2

M'Cheyne's Communion with God

Chapter 6

---- ❦ ----

Communion with God
by His Word

A calm hour with God is worth a whole lifetime
with man.

—ROBERT MURRAY M'CHEYNE, *Memoir and
Remains of Robert Murray M'Cheyne*

Robert Murray M'Cheyne believed there was no greater privilege
in life than communion with God. His desire for all-surpassing
fellowship with the Lord determined how he spent his time during his few years on earth.

While M'Cheyne had a number of close friends with whom
he enjoyed fellowship, his desire for fellowship with Christ sur-
passed them all. His sermon notes from a message on the Song
of Solomon 8:13–14 compare earthly friends with Christ: "They
are but cisterns—Christ is the fountain. They are but candles—
Christ is the sun. They are but creatures—Christ is the creator.
We must leave them, and betake ourselves to him."[1] In his notes
for a lecture on the ten virgins (Matt. 25:10–13), he wrote: "The
greatest joy of a believer in this world is to enjoy the presence of
Christ—not seen, not felt, not heard, but still real—the real presence of the unseen Saviour."[2]

---

1. Robert Murray M'Cheyne, *From the Preacher's Heart* (1846; repr., Geanies
House, Scotland: Christian Focus, 1993), 216.
2. M'Cheyne, *From the Preacher's Heart*, 466.

People seek discipline in their devotional lives for varied reasons. Some want more biblical knowledge. Others seek peace for the day ahead. But for M'Cheyne, it was love of God that compelled him to spend time with his Lord. His diary entry of February 23, 1834, reads, "Rose early to seek God, and found Him whom my soul loveth. Who would not rise early to meet such company?"[3] When love for God motivates our prayer, study, and worship, a sense of duty will be replaced by a sense of delight. Then time with God can be viewed as both privilege and pleasure. M'Cheyne wrote, "Are we to have no pleasure, then? Yes, in Christ—holy pleasures, such as are at God's right hand for evermore. Ah! I have tasted all the pleasures of time, and they are not worth one drop of Christ's sweet love."[4]

M'Cheyne, a tireless worker despite his poor health, gave his first and best hours of the day to fellowship with the Lord. Biographer Alexander Smellie writes:

> His first concern was the nurture of his soul. Every morning he saw to it before he turned to anything else. He rose early that he might have time to spend with God. Probably he had gone to bed at a late hour of the night, jaded in body and mind after a day of duty.... He would sing a Psalm, to tune his spirit into harmony with heavenly things. Then he sat down to read, mark, learn, and inwardly digest the living Word of his Lord, often studying three chapters in succession. Then he gave himself to prayer, the effectual prayer which avails much. And he was more refreshed than if he had prolonged the hours of sleep; he was furnished and prepared for every good work.[5]

M'Cheyne's love for communion with God was directly related to his love for the Sabbath day. Though he exerted much

3. Andrew A. Bonar, *Memoir and Remains of Robert Murray M'Cheyne* (1844; repr., Edinburgh: Banner of Truth, 2004), 23.

4. M'Cheyne, *From the Preacher's Heart*, 350.

5. Alexander Smellie, *Robert Murray M'Cheyne* (1913; repr., Geanies House, Scotland: Christian Focus, 1995), 73.

energy in preaching on Sundays, his custom was to spend additional hours in prayer and meditation on the Sabbath. L. J. Van Valen writes about M'Cheyne's devotional practice, "On the Sabbath he followed a different schedule; he made use of seven periods, in total six hours, for studying the Scriptures and for prayer."[6] Even though M'Cheyne rose early and stayed up late in order to have additional time alone with God on Sabbath days, his was not a legalistic motivation. A friend wrote to him with the unusual question as to whether it was sinful to spend time registering meteorological observations on the Sabbath (evidently a pleasurable hobby for some in 1842). M'Cheyne's reply tells us much about his delight in the Sabbath day:

> I love the Lord's Day too well to be marking down the height of the thermometer and barometer every hour. I have other work to do, higher and better, and more like that of angels above. The more entirely I can give my Sabbaths to God, and half forget that I am not before the throne of the Lamb, with my harp of gold, the happier I am, and I feel it my duty to be as happy as I can be, and as God intended me to be. The joy of the Lord is my strength.... This is the noblest science, to know how to live in hourly communion with God in Christ.[7]

M'Cheyne's love for communion with God was observed by many people throughout his brief life. One of the most interesting observations came from an elderly servant of M'Cheyne's good friend Andrew Bonar. M'Cheyne had visited his friend to preach in Collace, and Bonar's servant was struck by the devotional life of the great preacher. His words are preserved for us in *Reminiscences of Andrew Bonar D. D.*:

> Oh, to hear Mr. M'Cheyne at prayers in the mornin'! It was as if he could never gi'e ower, he had sae muckle to ask.

---

6. Leen J. Van Valen, *Constrained by His Love: A New Biography on Robert Murray McCheyne*, trans. Laurence R. Noculson (Geanies House, Scotland: Christian Focus, 2002), 157.

7. A. Bonar, *Memoir and Remains*, 140–42.

Ye would hae thocht the very walls would speak again. He used to rise at six on the Sabbath mornin,' and go to bed at twelve at night, for he said he likit to have the whole day alone with God.[8]

M'Cheyne labored intensely in preaching and visiting among the four thousand people in the parish of St. Peter's. But, in the words of Andrew Bonar, "He felt meditation and prayer to be the very sinews of his work."[9] M'Cheyne knew that the source of his strength for ministry was his communion with God. He made it his first and most valued work—"I ought to spend the best hours of the day in communion with God. It is my noblest and most fruitful employment, and is not to be thrust into any corner."[10]

Delight in God's Word

> All my ideas of peace and joy are linked in with my Bible, and I would not give the hours of secret converse with it for all the other hours I spend in this world.
>
> —ROBERT MURRAY M'CHEYNE, *Memoir and Remains of Robert Murray M'Cheyne*

For M'Cheyne, the Bible was the starting place for his fellowship with God. It was also the sustenance for his spiritual growth. He knew that, as a pastor, he must first be nurtured by God's Word before he could lead others toward growth in faith. Before he left for the Holy Land, he wrote these words to W. C. Burns, the man who would preach at St. Peter's during his absence:

> Take heed to yourself. Your own soul is your first and greatest care. You know a sound body alone can work with power; much more a healthy soul. Keep a clear conscience through the blood of the Lamb. Keep up close communion with God.

---

8. Marjory Bonar, *Reminiscences of Andrew A. Bonar D. D.* (London: Hodder and Stoughton, 1897), 9.

9. A. Bonar, *Memoir and Remains*, 56.

10. A. Bonar, *Memoir and Remains*, 158.

Study likeness to him in all things. Read the Bible for your own growth first, then for your people.[11]

M'Cheyne's love for God was expressed in love for His Word, and he viewed God's Word as an instrument that conveyed God's love to him. In a sermon entitled "The Pilgrim's Staff," M'Cheyne said, "And this makes the Bible not a book written for one, but a book written to me—a letter by the Lord, and directed to me; and therefore every word of divine love and tenderness that he has written in this book belongs to me."[12] To him, Scripture was not only an instrument that conveyed God's love but also one that brought His sanctifying grace. His sermon notes for a message on the Song of Solomon 5:2–16 read, "In the daily reading of the Word, Christ pays daily visits to sanctify the believing soul."[13]

M'Cheyne's morning devotional time regularly included the reading of three chapters of Scripture, and on Sundays he customarily reviewed the chapters he had read during the week. In addition to his daily devotional reading of Scripture, M'Cheyne spent significant time in Bible study, and his sermons, letters, and diary entries all attest to a remarkable knowledge of Scripture. In a letter he wrote from the Holy Land to his friend Rev. Robert S. Candlish, M'Cheyne included twenty-eight allusions to biblical passages or direct quotations of Scripture. Twenty-one of these were from the Old Testament, and most were related to locations M'Cheyne and his party had visited. His knowledge of obscure details and locations mentioned in this letter points to an extraordinary familiarity with the Bible.[14]

M'Cheyne knew well the more obscure parts of the Bible and felt very free to preach on them. He believed we should study the

---

11. Michael D. McMullen, *God's Polished Arrow: William Chalmers Burns* (Geanies House, Scotland: Christian Focus, 2000), 29.

12. Robert M. M'Cheyne, *A Basket of Fragments* (1848; repr., Geanies House, Scotland: Christian Focus, 2001), 179.

13. M'Cheyne, *From the Preacher's Heart*, 232.

14. Robert M. M'Cheyne, *Familiar Letters by the Rev. Robert Murray M'Cheyne* (1848; repr., Charleston, S.C.: Bibliolife, 2009), 106–20.

entirety of Scripture without neglecting any part, noting "we must not pass over 'hard' things, though in the Bible, but read them with prayer and holy reverence, looking up to God for the enlightening influence of the Holy Ghost."[15]

M'Cheyne not only read and studied Scripture, he memorized it as well. In a letter to his flock while traveling through Poland, he wrote, "All our Bibles were taken away from us, even our Hebrew ones, that we might not preach to the Jews the glad tidings of a Saviour. Blessed be God, they could not take them from our memories and hearts."[16]

Though his knowledge of Scripture was remarkable, M'Cheyne never lost his thirst to know more. Even in the final year of his life, after having preached hundreds of biblical sermons, he longed to know how to study the Bible more effectively. In a letter dated August 18, 1842 (just seven months before he died), M'Cheyne wrote to Horace (Horatius) Bonar, "I have great desire for personal growth in faith and holiness. I love the word of God, and find it sweetest nourishment to my soul. Can you help me to study it more successfully?"[17]

As a pastor, M'Cheyne also wanted his flock to study the Bible successfully, and just three months before he died, he provided the members of St. Peter's with a daily Bible reading plan. In a letter to his church dated December 30, 1842, he wrote: "It has long been in my mind to prepare a scheme of Scripture reading, in which as many as were made willing by God might agree, so that the whole Bible might be read once by you in the year, and all might be feeding in the same portion of the green pasture at the same time."[18]

M'Cheyne's Bible reading plan actually guides a reader through the New Testament and the Psalms twice, and the rest of the Bible once in each year. Presented in calendar form, it provides readings

---

15. Kirkwood Hewat, *M'Cheyne from the Pew: Being Extracts from the Diary of William Lamb* (London: S. W. Partridge, n.d.), 37.

16. A. Bonar, *Memoir and Remains*, 261.

17. A. Bonar, *Memoir and Remains*, 313–14.

18. A. Bonar, *Memoir and Remains*, 619.

for both family and "secret," or personal, devotional times each day.[19] M'Cheyne had several reasons for encouraging his church to follow this plan. First, his members would read the entire Bible in an orderly manner each year. Further, both he and the elders would know what parts of Scripture their members were reading each day, which could help facilitate ministry to them in house-to-house visitation. M'Cheyne also believed that love and unity would be strengthened in his church as members read the same passages of Scripture each day, writing, "We shall oftener be led to agree on earth, touching something we shall ask of God. We shall pray over the same promises, mourn over the same confessions, praise God in the same songs, and be nourished by the same words of eternal life."[20]

But M'Cheyne's greatest hope for his church was that they would come to know the benefits of God's Word as he had. He wrote to them, "Above all, use the Word as a lamp to your feet and a light to your path—your guide in perplexity, your armour in temptation, your food in times of faintness. Hear the constant cry of the great Intercessor, 'Sanctify Them through Thy Truth: Thy Word Is Truth.'"[21]

M'Cheyne's own reliance upon Scripture as a lamp to his feet and light to his path is perhaps best expressed in this poem, titled "Thy Word Is a Lamp unto My Feet, and Light unto My Path," which he wrote in 1838:

> When Israel knew not where to go,
> God made the fiery pillar glow;
> By night, by day, above the camp
> It led the way—their guiding lamp:
> Such is Thy holy word to me
> In day of dark perplexity.
> When devious paths before me spread,

19. Robert Murray M'Cheyne, "Read the Bible in a Year" (1842; repr., Edinburgh: Banner of Truth Trust, 1998).

20. A. Bonar, *Memoir and Remains*, 621.

21. A. Bonar, *Memoir and Remains*, 622.

And all invite my foot to tread,
I hear Thy voice behind me say—
"Believing soul, this is the way;
Walk thou in it." O gentle Dove,
How much Thy holy law I love!
    My lamp and light
    In the dark night.

When Paul amid the seas seemed lost,
By Adrian billows wildly tossed,
When neither sun nor star appeared,
And every wave its white head reared
Above the ship, beside his bed
An angel stood, and "Fear not" said.
Such is Thy holy word to me
When tossed upon affliction's sea:
When floods come in unto my soul,
And the deep waters o'er me roll,
With angel voice Thy word draws near
And says, "'Tis I, why shouldst thou fear?
Through troubles great My saints must go
Into their rest, where neither woe
Nor sin can come; where every tear
From off the cheek shall disappear,
Wiped by God's hand." O gentle Dove,
Thy holy law how much I love!
    My lamp and light
    In the dark night.

When holy Stephen dauntless stood
Before the Jews, who sought his blood.
With angel face he looked on high,
And wondering, through the parted sky,
Saw Jesus risen from His throne
To claim the martyr as His own.
Angelic peace that sight bestowed,
With holy joy his bosom glowed;
And while the murderous stones they hurled,
His heaven-wrapt soul sought yonder world

Of rest. "My spirit, Saviour, keep,"
He cried, he kneeled, he fell asleep.
Such be thy holy word to me
In hour of life's extremity!
Although no more the murdering hand
Is raised within our peaceful land—
The Church has rest, and I may ne'er
Be called the martyr's crown to wear:
Yet still, in whatsoever form
Death comes to me—in midnight storm
Whelming my bark, or in my nest,
Gently dismissing me to rest,—
O grant me in Thy word to see
A risen Saviour beckoning me.
No evil then my heart shall fear
In the dark valley. Thou art near!
My trembling soul and Thou, my God,
Alone are there; Thy staff and rod
Shall comfort me. O gentle Dove,
How much Thy holy law I love!
    My lamp and light
    In the dark night.[22]

22. A. Bonar, *Memoir and Remains*, 640.

Chapter 7

———————— ❦ ————————

Communion with God in Prayer

I am persuaded that I ought never to do anything without prayer, and, if possible, special, secret [private] prayer.

—ROBERT MURRAY M'CHEYNE, *Memoir and Remains of Robert Murray M'Cheyne*

Robert Murray M'Cheyne was, above all things, a man of prayer. His love for prayer grew out of his understanding that prayer was communion with God—an all-surpassing fellowship to be treasured and prioritized. A person who came to him for counsel recalled, "He told me to take everything to Jesus, however small, just as I did to him, for He is not only able to help you, but He loves to have communion and fellowship with those He loves."[1]

This understanding of the purpose of prayer—that it is both for obtaining help and for communion—is often neglected. Most Christians focus only on the value of prayer for obtaining help, and the provision of such help may indeed be for the glory of God and the advancement of His kingdom. But if we focus only on the need for answers to prayer, we will miss much of the privilege God has given us in prayer. M'Cheyne knew that prayer was to be

———————————

1. J. C. Smith, *Robert Murray M'Cheyne: A Good Minister of Jesus Christ* (1870; repr., Belfast, Ireland: Ambassador Productions, 2002), 163–64.

enjoyed as communion with God. While preparing for a sermon entitled "The Soul of the Believer a Garden," he noted:

> But communion with Christ is always sanctifying. Oh! It is good for the soul to meet with Jesus. Oh! If you would go to Jesus and tell him all, if you would cause him to hear it, how much happier lives you would lead! Let there be the utmost frankness between your soul and Christ. Cover no sin before him; pour out every joy; unbosom every grief; seek counsel in every perplexity.[2]

M'Cheyne's understanding of prayer as communion with Christ caused him to view prayer as the greatest of privileges. In prayer, a believer not only seeks God's provision but also His person. Prayer does not merely link us to God's resources; it allows us to experience His presence.

M'Cheyne was especially conscious of God's presence with him during times of prayer and understood that all three persons of the Trinity—Father, Son, and Holy Spirit—are involved with us when we pray. In a Communion service address in 1841, M'Cheyne said, "When a believer prays, he is not alone—there are three with him: the Father seeing in secret, His ear open; the Son blotting out sin, and offering up the prayer; the Holy Ghost quickening and giving desires."[3] This awareness of God's presence in prayer enabled M'Cheyne to see prayer as "a sweet well of delight."[4]

Prayer and Power

While M'Cheyne understood the privilege of prayer as fellowship with God, he did not underestimate its immense value in furthering the work of God's kingdom. In fact, M'Cheyne viewed prayer as the first and most important work in advancing God's

---

2. Robert Murray M'Cheyne, *From the Preacher's Heart* (1846; repr., Geanies House, Scotland: Christian Focus, 1993), 216–17.

3. Andrew A. Bonar, *Memoir and Remains of Robert Murray M'Cheyne* (1844; repr., Edinburgh: Banner of Truth, 2004), 509.

4. M'Cheyne, *From the Preacher's Heart*, 223.

purposes. His sermon notes for a message entitled "I Will Pour Water" read, "We are often for preaching to awaken others; but we should be more concerned with prayer. Prayer is more powerful than preaching. It is prayer that gives preaching all its power."[5] For another message, he noted, "Prayer must be added to preaching, else preaching is in vain." Later in the same message, his notes read, "O believing brethren, what an instrument is this which God hath put into your hands! Prayer moves him that moves the universe."[6]

It was this high view of prayer that shaped M'Cheyne's perspective as to what was most important in his ministry. When he was required to temporarily withdraw from his pastorate due to his health, he saw this as an opportunity to pray more for his church. On February 6, 1839, he wrote these words to his members: "Another mark of His loving kindness to us is His suffering me to pray for you. You remember how the Apostles describe the work of the ministry: 'We will give ourselves continually to prayer, and to the ministry of the Word' (Acts 6:4)."[7] It was also during this time of absence from his pastorate that he wrote to his friend Rev. R. MacDonald of Blairgowrie: "I am persuaded that I have been brought into retirement to teach me the value and need of prayer. Alas! I have not estimated aright the value of near access unto God."[8]

A Pattern for Prayer

M'Cheyne's pattern for daily prayer is revealed in personal notes that he titled "Reformation in Secret Prayer."[9] Here, he notes that his daily prayer should include confession of sin, adoration, thanksgiving, petition, and intercession. He goes on to specify a long list of those for whom he should intercede, including his

5. M'Cheyne, *From the Preacher's Heart*, 83.

6. M'Cheyne, *From the Preacher's Heart*, 277, 279.

7. Robert Murray M'Cheyne, *Pastoral Letters* (1844; repr., Shoals, Ind.: Kingsley, 2003), 22.

8. A. Bonar, *Memoir and Remains*, 209–10.

9. A. Bonar, *Memoir and Remains*, 156–58.

family, friends, flock, the Church of Scotland, and missionaries. While he noted that we cannot "reckon communion with God by minutes or hours, or by solitude," he did seek to prioritize his times of prayer. He wrote, "In general, it is best to have at least one hour alone with God, before engaging in anything else." He wrote further, "I ought to pray before seeing anyone." M'Cheyne's rule was "to begin with God—to see His face first—to get my soul near Him before it is near another."[10]

M'Cheyne believed in the value of a pattern—some structure to guide us in daily prayer. And he believed in the value of having a designated time and place to pray as well. In a lecture on John 11 (the story of Mary, Martha, and Lazarus), he said:

> If you are a child of God, you will find some secret place to pray. It will not do to say, you will pray when walking, or at your work, or in the midst of company. It will not do to make that your praying time through the day. No; Satan is at your right hand. Get alone with God. Spend as much time as you can alone with God every day; and then, in sudden temptations and afflictions, you will be able to lift your heart easily even among the crowd to your Father's ear.[11]

The Spirit and the Word

While embracing the importance of a plan, a place, and a time for daily prayer, M'Cheyne knew that discipline alone could not make prayer effective but that it was necessary to have the help of the Holy Spirit. In a sermon entitled "Grieve Not the Spirit," he spoke of the friendship that exists between the Holy Spirit and the Christian:

> So, brethren, this is another mark of the Holy Spirit's friend-ship, that he not only dwells in the soul, but he teaches the soul to say, "Abba"—he teaches the soul to "pray in the Holy Ghost." It is true friendship to teach one another to pray. It is a believing mother's part to teach her little children to

10. A. Bonar, *Memoir and Remains*, 156–57.
11. M'Cheyne, *From the Preacher's Heart*, 502.

pray. But the Holy Spirit's love is greater than this, he not only puts the words in our mouth, but he puts the desire in our heart. It is great friendship to pray together; but oh! It is greatest friendship to pray in one, and this is the friendship of the Spirit of God.[12]

While M'Cheyne believed that our prayers should be enabled by the Holy Spirit, he also believed they should be shaped by Scripture. In a letter to Mr. J. T. Just about how to conduct prayer meetings, he wrote, "Let your prayers in the meeting be formed as much as possible upon what you have read in the Bible. You will thus learn a variety of petition, and a Scripture style."[13] To another, he wrote: "Turn the Bible into prayer. Thus, if you are reading the first psalm, spread the Bible on the chair before you, and kneel and pray: 'O Lord, give me the blessedness of the man,' etc.; 'Let me not stand in the counsel of the ungodly,' etc. This is the best way of knowing the meaning of the Bible and of learning to pray."[14]

When prayers were based upon clear biblical promises, M'Cheyne believed the one praying should have faith that those prayers would be answered. While he strongly believed in the complete sovereignty of God, he also believed the Christian was responsible for putting faith in God's promises in order to see God's answers. Thus, he could write to his church, "Oh, there is nothing that I would love you to be more sure of than this: that God hears and answers prayer. There never was and never will be a believing prayer left unanswered."[15] In the first of seven lectures on John 11, M'Cheyne said, "Learn that urgency in prayer does not so much consist in vehement pleadings, as in vehement believing. He that believes most the love and power of Jesus will obtain most in prayer."[16]

---

12. Robert M. M'Cheyne, *A Basket of Fragments* (1848; repr., Geanies House, Scotland: Christian Focus, 2001), 159–62.

13. A. Bonar, *Memoir and Remains*, 275–76.

14. Smith, *Robert Murray M'Cheyne*, 66.

15. M'Cheyne, *Pastoral Letters*, 38.

16. M'Cheyne, *From the Preacher's Heart*, 475.

Intercessory Prayer

M'Cheyne believed that, as a pastor, he was especially called to intercessory prayer for the members of his own church. Biographer Alexander Smellie describes a notebook he kept with details about how he prayed for those in his congregation. He divided the people into eleven categories, such as the "careless," the "anxious," and the "Christians" (those whose faith was not in doubt).[17] He regularly prayed for those in each category.

M'Cheyne looked to Jesus as his model in intercessory prayer. In his notes about his own "Personal Reformation," he wrote, "I ought to study Christ as Intercessor. He prayed most for Peter, who was to be most tempted. I am on His breastplate. If I could hear Christ praying for me in the next room, I would not fear a million of enemies. Yet the distance makes no difference; He is praying for me."[18]

With Christ the Intercessor as his example, M'Cheyne prayed not only for his own flock but for other pastors and churches as well. Early in his pastoral ministry, he joined with Andrew Bonar and other pastors in a commitment to pray for each other on Saturday evenings. Bonar later wrote that "Mr. M'Cheyne never failed to remember this time of prayer."[19]

M'Cheyne's exceptional prayer life was not limited to his personal times of prayer. He was well aware of the power of united prayer and often met with others to pray. After returning from his mission trip to Israel, he became part of a ministerial prayer meeting in Dundee, coming together with other pastors for an hour and a half on Monday afternoons to pray together for each other and for their churches. M'Cheyne rarely missed these meetings.[20]

Soon after his ordination as pastor at St. Peter's, M'Cheyne began a Thursday evening prayer meeting at the church. Hundreds

---

17. Alexander Smellie, *Robert Murray M'Cheyne* (1913; repr., Geanies House, Scotland: Christian Focus, 1995),128–29.

18. A. Bonar, *Memoir and Remains*, 154.

19. A. Bonar, *Memoir and Remains*, 52.

20. A. Bonar, *Memoir and Remains*, 129.

of members regularly came to this gathering, in which M'Cheyne would typically do a short teaching, often concerning a promise from Scripture regarding the outpouring of God's Spirit. He also read brief accounts from revival history.[21] Alexander Smellie writes:

> The Thursday prayer meeting was a new thing in the religion of the town. It was so large that it was held in the church itself; we read of eight hundred as sometimes attending. A special benediction rested on it; the wings of the Spirit lay close and warm then about the speaker and hearers.[22]

Regarding the Thursday prayer meeting, author John Shearer writes of M'Cheyne, "Here he read to his people or told them the story of God's marvelous work in past revivals. Once again, as so often before and since, the seed of the great harvest was sown in the prayer meeting."[23]

Not only was the "seed" sown in the Thursday prayer meeting, but the revival for which M'Cheyne longed and prayed sprouted there as well. It happened in August 1839, while he was still away during the mission to Israel. At the time, he was sick and confined to bed, yet praying with what strength he had for his church in Dundee. W. C. Burns had returned to St. Peter's to lead the Thursday night prayer meeting, and he shared of the outpouring of God's Spirit he had recently witnessed in Kilsyth. Burns invited those at St. Peter's who felt "the need of an outpouring of the Spirit to convert them" to stay past the end of the meeting. About one hundred people stayed. As Burns spoke to them, God's power descended, and "all were bathed in tears." A meeting was held Friday with similar results: "It was like a pent-up flood breaking forth; tears were streaming from the eyes of many, and some fell on the ground groaning, and weeping, and crying for mercy."[24] Meetings

---

21. A. Bonar, *Memoir and Remains*, 62.

22. Smellie, *Robert Murray M'Cheyne*, 62.

23. John Shearer, *Old Time Revivals* (Philadelphia: Million Testaments Campaign, 1932), 65.

24. A. Bonar, *Memoir and Remains*, 114.

continued for many weeks after that night, and the entire city of Dundee was affected. Dr. Michael McMullen, in his biography of W. C. Burns, writes: "Burns himself tells us the church was so crowded every night many had to be turned away and that after every service there were throngs of people remaining behind for prayer and counsel."[25]

M'Cheyne's prayers for revival had been answered, remarkably, while he was away from his church. M'Cheyne would not be able to return to St. Peter's until November, and William Burns continued preaching regularly until that time. Sensitive to the fact that he was a guest in the pulpit, Burns was relieved to know that M'Cheyne celebrated the outpouring that began under his preaching. An extract from Burns's journal, dated November 15, 1839, reads:

> Had a letter from dear Mr. M'Cheyne written in a spirit of joy for the work of the Lord, which shows a great triumph, I think, of divine grace over the natural jealousy of the human heart. O Lord, I would praise thee with all my heart for this, and would entreat that when thy dear servant, the pastor of this people, is restored to them, he may be honoured a hundredfold more in winning souls to Christ than I have been in thine infinite and sovereign mercy. Amen.[26]

M'Cheyne's joy at hearing of the revival in his absence was surely due in part to the many prayers he had prayed for revival to come to St. Peter's. He had taught his church to pray for revival as well. In a sermon entitled "Thy People Shall Be Willing" (Psalm 110:3), he said, "Oh, for a day of his power! Oh, long for such a day! Another Pentecost! I charge you, pray for it. Set apart peculiar times for preparing for it."[27] His prayers and those of his church

25. Michael D. McMullen, *God's Polished Arrow: William Chalmers Burns* (Geanies House, Scotland: Christian Focus, 2000), 36.

26. McMullen, *God's Polished Arrow*, 164.

27. Robert Murray M'Cheyne, *The Passionate Preacher: Sermons of Robert Murray M'Cheyne*, ed. Michael D. McMullen (Geanies House, Scotland: Christian Focus, 1999), 26.

were answered, and he was able to celebrate this, even though he was not the one in the pulpit when the answers came.

The revival did, however, continue at St. Peter's after M'Cheyne's return. One result of the outpouring of God's Spirit was an even greater engagement in prayer. M'Cheyne found thirty-nine different prayer meetings underway at St. Peter's when he returned. Five of these were conducted and attended by children.[28] The prayers of M'Cheyne and his congregation were both an impetus for revival and the fruit of that revival.

Since M'Cheyne lived such a remarkable life of prayer, it should be no surprise that many of his last recorded words were prayers for his people. L. J. Van Valen notes that on one occasion, when near death, M'Cheyne prayed without ceasing for two hours for his congregation, especially interceding for those not yet converted.[29]

In his short life, M'Cheyne had learned a very valuable truth: "Unless the LORD builds the house, they labor in vain who build it" (Ps. 127:1). He was a remarkably disciplined and diligent worker, but he knew that human effort could not build God's church. Jesus Christ alone can build His church, and He uses the prayers of His people to do it. His understanding of this great truth is perhaps best seen in an excerpt from a letter to his good friend Alex Somerville. M'Cheyne wrote, "Do not overwork yourself. There is much of self in that, I know by experience. A breathing of believing prayer may be worth many hours' hard labor."[30]

---

28. A. Bonar, *Memoir and Remains*, 544–45.

29. Leen J. Van Valen, *Constrained by His Love: A New Biography on Robert Murray McCheyne*, trans. Laurence R. Noculson (Geanies House, Scotland: Christian Focus, 2002), 418.

30. Robert M. M'Cheyne, *Familiar Letters by the Rev. Robert Murray M'Cheyne* (1848; repr., Charleston, S.C.: Bibliolife, 2009), 195.

Chapter 8

The Joy of Holiness

Seek to be made holier every day. Pray, strive, wrestle for the Spirit to make you like God. Be as much as you can with God.

—Robert Murray M'Cheyne, *Pastoral Letters*

An essential part of Robert Murray M'Cheyne's communion with God was his ongoing pursuit of holiness. His desire to be made more holy was not a legalistic quest to be assured of his salvation. Rather, knowing that he had been freely justified by faith in Christ resulted in love that led to holiness. In his sermon notes for a message entitled "The Love of Christ," M'Cheyne wrote, "Forgiven much, you will love much. Loving much, you will live to the service of him whom you love. This is the grand master-principle of which we spoke; this is the secret spring of all the holiness of the saints."[1]

In M'Cheyne's view, the great key to growth in holiness was reliance upon the Holy Spirit. In his sermon "Grieve Not the Spirit," he made the point that we grieve the Spirit when we do not lean upon Him:

When you do not take all your holiness from him. This is the great work of the Spirit in you, to make you holy.... Now,

———————

1. Robert Murray M'Cheyne, *From the Preacher's Heart* (1846; repr., Geanies House, Scotland: Christian Focus, 1993), 53.

when temptations and trials, and lusts come crowding in, if we do not lean upon the Spirit, we grieve him. Or, if we lean upon another, if you lean upon your education, your good resolutions, your past experiences. Or, suppose you run into temptation, and say, I was well brought up, I am able to resist it. In these ways you grieve the Spirit.[2]

M'Cheyne himself made what we might call "resolutions," but he termed his quest for greater sanctification "Reformation." In his "Personal Reformation," he wrote down his commitment to seek God's sanctifying work in his life. It begins:

> I am persuaded that I shall obtain the highest amount of present happiness, I shall do most for God's glory and the good of man, and I shall have the fullest reward in eternity, by maintaining a conscience always washed in Christ's blood, by being filled with the Holy Spirit at all times, and by attaining the most entire likeness to Christ in mind, will, and heart, that is possible for a redeemed sinner to attain to in this world.[3]

His "Personal Reformation" goes on to reveal a great determination to recognize sin in his life and confess it as promptly as possible. He wrote, "I am persuaded that I ought to confess my sins more. I think I ought to confess sin the moment I see it to be a sin; whether I am in company, or in study, or even preaching, the soul ought to cast a glance of abhorrence at the sin."[4] In order to better recognize sin in his life, M'Cheyne felt he needed to have special, set-apart times for that very purpose. He wrote, "I ought to have a stated day of confession, with fasting—say, once a month."[5]

M'Cheyne was cautious about thinking he had gained victory over temptation or was immune to the lure of sin. Concerning

---

2. Robert M. M'Cheyne, *A Basket of Fragments* (1848; repr., Geanies House, Scotland: Christian Focus, 2001), 164.

3. Andrew A. Bonar, *Memoir and Remains of Robert Murray M'Cheyne* (1844; repr., Edinburgh: Banner of Truth, 2004), 150.

4. A. Bonar, *Memoir and Remains*, 15.

5. A. Bonar, *Memoir and Remains*, 15.

this, his Reformation reads, "I am tempted to think that I am now an established Christian,—that I have overcome this or that lust so long,—that I have got into the habit of the opposite grace,—so that there is no fear; I may venture very near the temptation— nearer than other men. This is a lie of Satan."[6]

M'Cheyne's determined pursuit of holiness may sound overly introspective to some, but he was not relying upon himself to recognize or overcome sin. His reliance was upon the Holy Spirit. He wrote, "I am helpless in respect of every lust that ever was, or ever will be, in the human heart.... My only safety is to know, feel, and confess my helplessness, that I may hang upon the arm of Omnipotence.... but the main defense is casting myself into the arms of Christ like a helpless child, and beseeching Him to fill me with the Holy Spirit."[7] Knowing that the Lord alone could make him holy, he continued in his Reformation:

> I ought to study the Comforter more,—His Godhead, His love, His Almightiness. I have found by experience that nothing sanctifies me so much as meditating on the Comforter.... I ought never to forget that my body is dwelt in by the third Person of the Godhead. The very thought of this should make me tremble to sin. (1 Cor. vi)[8]

In his quest for holiness, M'Cheyne also knew that the Bible was essential. He saw God as the author of sanctification and His Word as the sanctifying instrument. In a message entitled "The Heavenly Bridegroom and Bride," he said:

> Learn the means of sanctification—the Word. No holiness without the Bible! I believe God could sanctify without the Word. He made the angels holy without it, and he made Adam holy without it, but He will not do it. "Sanctify them through the truth, Thy Word is truth" (John 17:17).... Learn,

---

6. A. Bonar, *Memoir and Remains*, 152.

7. A. Bonar, *Memoir and Remains*, 153–54.

8. A. Bonar, *Memoir and Remains*, 154.

then, that there is no other means of sanctification, and without holiness no man shall see the Lord.[9]

M'Cheyne's personal pursuit of holiness undoubtedly shaped his preaching. His sermons and sermon notes reveal that holiness was one of the topics most often stressed in his messages. L. J. Van Valen writes about M'Cheyne as a preacher: "The great secret of his proclamation is 'holiness.' He not only practiced, but also emphasized this aspect to a greater degree than most other teachers of the Scottish church."[10] M'Cheyne did not believe that holiness was optional for those who were genuinely converted and often stressed that "without holiness, no man can see God."[11]

For M'Cheyne, the pursuit of a holy life was evidence that a person was genuinely converted. In a message called "Tasting and Growing," he said, "Dear Christians, the only true mark of *life* is *growth*.... Oh! Ask the Lord that you may grow: grow in faith, in peace, in holiness."[12]

M'Cheyne's belief that genuine faith was characterized by the fruit of holiness is illustrated in the closing lines of his poem "The Barren Fig Tree":

> Learn, O my soul, what God demands
> Is not a faith like barren sands,
> But fruit of heavenly hue.
> By this we prove that Christ we know,
> If in His holy steps we go:
> Faith works by love, if true.[13]

---

9. M'Cheyne, *Basket of Fragments*, 91.

10. Leen J. Van Valen, *Constrained by His Love: A New Biography on Robert Murray McCheyne*, trans. Laurence R. Noculson (Geanies House, Scotland: Christian Focus, 2002), 477.

11. Robert Murray M'Cheyne, *New Testament Sermons*, ed. Michael D. McMullen (Edinburgh: Banner of Truth, 2004), 230.

12. M'Cheyne, *New Testament Sermons*, 257.

13. A. Bonar, *Memoir and Remains*, 632.

Joy in Holiness

For M'Cheyne, holiness was not just the fruit of genuine faith. It was his greatest joy. In his Reformation he wrote, "I am persuaded that God's happiness is inseparably linked in with His holiness. Holiness and happiness are like light and heat.... The redeemed, through all eternity, will never taste one of the pleasures of sin; yet their happiness is complete. It would be my greatest happiness to be from this moment entirely like them. Every sin is something away from my greatest enjoyment.[14] M'Cheyne summarized his view of holiness in a simple statement found in one of his letters to a friend: "There is no joy like that of holiness."[15]

His pursuit of holiness and his deep humility both sprang from his high view of God. M'Cheyne had a strong sense of his own unworthiness before God. And he marveled that God would use him despite his sinfulness. While absent from his congregation during a time of illness, he wrote to them:

> I am indeed amazed that the ministry of such a worm as I should even have been blessed among you at all; and I do this day bewail before you every sin in my heart and life that has kept back the light from your poor dark souls. Oh, you that can pray, pray that I may come back a holy minister, a shepherd to lead the flock not by the voice only, but to walk before them in the way of life.[16]

In M'Cheyne, we see the reality that close communion with God makes us more aware of our own need. A clearer view of His holiness gives a clearer view of our sinfulness. The closer we grow to Christ, the more we see our need of Christ. This awareness of our need gives us a greater gratitude for the gift of righteousness through Jesus.

---

14. A. Bonar, *Memoir and Remains*, 154.
15. A. Bonar, *Memoir and Remains*, 277.
16. Robert Murray M'Cheyne, *Pastoral Letters* (1844; repr., Shoals, Ind.: Kingsley, 2003), 70–71.

Observable Holiness

M'Cheyne's holiness was often observable to others. Many have referred to the "saintly" M'Cheyne and have recalled the holy influence of his life.[17] Those who knew him seem to agree that a beautiful sense of holiness flowed from his communion with God. David Yeaworth writes, "The key to McCheyne's ministerial success lay in his personal holiness and its manifestation to those around him."[18]

One of those who was around him most was his friend Andrew Bonar. In his *Memoir*, Bonar writes of M'Cheyne:

> His eminently holy walk and conversation, combined with the deep solemnity of his preaching, was specially felt. The people loved to speak of him. In one place, where a meeting had been intimated, the people assembled, resolving to cast stones at him as soon as he should begin to speak; but no sooner had he begun, than his manner, his look, his words, riveted them all, and they listened with intense earnestness; and before he left the place, the people gathered round him, entreating him to stay and preach to them. One man, who had cast mud at him, was afterwards moved to tears on hearing of his death.[19]

Andrew Bonar himself was especially influenced by M'Cheyne's evident devotion and the closeness of his communion with Christ. Bonar reflected on the life of his friend in his own diary entry of March 27, 1843, just two days after M'Cheyne's death:

> Yesterday was truly solemn from morning to evening. I was able to preach composedly, but often at intervals, while the psalms were singing, and sometimes in prayer, the thought of Robert was overwhelming.... I must myself live nearer God, and find what he found.... His forgetfulness of all that was

17. David Victor Yeaworth, "Robert Murray M'Cheyne (1813–1843): A Study of an Early Nineteenth-Century Scottish Evangelical" (PhD diss., Edinburgh, 1957), 96.

18. Yeaworth, "Robert Murray M'Cheyne," 141.

19. A. Bonar, *Memoir and Remains*, 160.

not found to God's glory was remarkable, and there seemed never a time when he was not himself feeling the presence of God…. O that his mantle would fall upon me!… He was so reverent toward God, so full also in desire toward Him, whether in family prayer or at common ordinary meetings. He seemed never unprepared. His lamp was always burning, and his loins always girt. I never knew it otherwise, even when we were journeying in Palestine. Lord, grant me henceforth more holiness.[20]

Andrew Bonar always remembered his friend on March 25, the anniversary of his death. After a visit to St. Peter's Church in Dundee in 1873, some thirty years after M'Cheyne's death, Bonar wrote, "There is still some peculiar fragrance in the air round Robert M'Cheyne's tomb!"[21] In 1881, Bonar still remembered the holy sense of God's presence with M'Cheyne, and he wrote, "Oh, when shall I attain to the same holy sweetness and unction, and when shall I reach the deep fellowship with God which he used to manifest?"[22]

James Hamilton sent a letter to Robert's father, Adam M'Cheyne, after his son's death. In sharing his sympathy for the family's loss, Hamilton noted the remarkable influence of M'Cheyne's holy life:

I never knew one so instant in season and out of season, so impressed with the invisible realities, and so faithful in reproving sin and witnessing for Christ…. Love to Christ was the great secret of all his devotion and consistency…. His continual communion with God gave wonderful sacredness to his character; and during the week that he spent with us last November, it seemed as if there were a sanctity diffused through our dwelling.[23]

---

20. Marjory Bonar, *Andrew A. Bonar, D. D.—Diary and Letters* (London: Hodder and Stoughton, 1894), 102.

21. Marjory Bonar, *Reminiscences of Andrew A. Bonar D. D.* (London: Hodder and Stoughton, 1897), 12.

22. M. Bonar, *Reminiscences*, 13.

23. Alexander Smellie, *Robert Murray M'Cheyne* (1913; repr., Geanies House, Scotland: Christian Focus, 1995), 172–73.

It is important to note that his was not a legalistic holiness that communicated condemnation to those who did not share his views. On one occasion, M'Cheyne visited family and friends in Dumfriesshire, among whom were three of his cousins. The three young women were described as "destitute of vital godliness and hostile to evangelical religion," and they dubbed M'Cheyne "Perfection." But in a short time, the women were won over by his gracious personality. In him, they saw that faith in Christ was not an enslaving yoke but a life-giving relationship. During family worship one evening, one of the girls began sobbing aloud, and the others soon followed. All three became devoted Christians and recalled it was their cousin's holy influence that "struck them down."[24]

Dr. Stalker, of Glasgow, provides another account of the influence of M'Cheyne's presence on one who was antagonistic toward Christians:

> In Alexandria, Egypt, a lady happened to be staying at one of the hotels there. Something had irritated her, and she launched forth against professing Christians as just a lot of hypocrites. She could not believe any of them. They would cheat whenever and wherever they could.
>
> "Well," said one who was patiently listening to this tirade, "did you never in all your life see one Christian, *one* follower of the Lord Jesus you believed in?"
>
> There was a pause. Then the lady, in a calmer tone, said, "Yes, I saw one—a man—a minister, in this hotel, a tall, spare man, from Scotland. He was a man of God. I watched him, and felt that he was a genuine Christian. His very look did me good."
>
> That minister was Robert Murray M'Cheyne. His holy consistent life was telling in that hotel among people he had never seen before, and many whom likely he would never see again![25]

---

24. Kirkwood Hewat, *M'Cheyne from the Pew: Being Extracts from the Diary of William Lamb* (London: S. W. Partridge, n.d.), 81–82.

25. Hewat, *M'Cheyne from the Pew*, 129–30.

M'Cheyne himself believed that a Christian's holiness should be evident. In a sermon on Hebrews 3:16–19, he made the point that believers in Jesus have a preserving effect on their world by their holy example. He said, "The very face and holy ways of a meek, humble child of God makes the world shrink back. His face is like that of Moses on which the children of Israel could not look. So there is something of heaven about every believer."[26] In another message, he said, "And you cannot be in the company of a holy man without receiving your impressions from him."[27]

M'Cheyne believed that ministers, especially, should pursue and give evidence of holy lives. To Rev. Dan Edwards, he wrote, "Remember you are God's sword,—His instrument,—I trust a chosen vessel unto Him to bear His name. In great measure, according to the purity and perfections of the instrument, will be the success. It is not great talents God blesses so much as great likeness to Jesus. A holy minister is an awful weapon in the hand of God."[28] To another pastor, he wrote, "Study universal holiness of life. Your whole usefulness depends on this, for your sermons last but an hour or two, your life preaches all the week."[29]

One of M'Cheyne's most often cited remarks is, "The greatest need of my people is my own holiness."[30] It is clear that he understood the call from God's Word to be "a vessel for honor, sanctified and useful for the Master, prepared for every good work" (2 Tim. 2:21). By his communion with God, M'Cheyne became such a vessel.

---

26. Robert Murray M'Cheyne, *The Passionate Preacher: Sermons of Robert Murray M'Cheyne*, ed. Michael D. McMullen (Geanies House, Scotland: Christian Focus, 1999), 276.

27. M'Cheyne, *A Basket of Fragments*, 162.

28. A. Bonar, *Memoir and Remains*, 282.

29. David Robertson, *Awakening: The Life and Ministry of Robert Murray M'Cheyne* (Geanies House, Scotland: Christian Focus, 2010), 130.

30. Robertson, *Awakening: Life and Ministry*, 135.

Chapter 9

Eternal Perspective

> Live near to God, and so all things will appear to
> you little in comparison with eternal realities.
>
> —ROBERT MURRAY M'CHEYNE, *Memoir and*
> *Remains of Robert Murray M'Cheyne*

One of the things that resulted from M'Cheyne's close communion with God was his clear view of the reality of eternal things.
He lived, to a remarkable degree, with an eternal perspective
regarding life on earth. He saw life, with its choices, challenges,
pleasures, and opportunities, in light of eternity. This eternal perspective helped him to hold this world loosely and to pursue God's
kingdom with zealous determination.

M'Cheyne used as an envelope seal a picture of the sun setting
behind a mountaintop. His motto accompanied the seal with the
simple words: "The night cometh."[1] His motto comes from Jesus'
call, "I must work the works of Him who sent Me while it is day;
the night is coming, when no one can work" (John 9:4, emphasis
added). M'Cheyne's eternal perspective gave an urgency to his
work for the Lord. He often said to friends, "Live and labour now,

---

1. Kirkwood Hewat, *M'Cheyne from the Pew: Being Extracts from the Diary of
William Lamb* (London: S. W. Partridge, n.d.), 97.

so that, when you die you may be missed by man and accepted by God."[2]

The Thain family was close to M'Cheyne, and apparently, Mrs. Thain had encouraged the busy young minister to take a time of rest from his tireless preaching and ministry schedule. In a letter of reply, he wrote:

> You know how glad I would be of some such retreat as Elijah had by the brook of Cherith, where I might learn more of my own heart, and of my Bible, and of my God, where I might while away the summer hours in quiet meditation, or talking of His righteousness all the day long. But it is only said of *the dead* in the Lord that they rest from their labours; and I fear I must not think of resting till then. Time is short, my time especially, and souls are precious.[3]

M'Cheyne's mention of "my time" here was apparently due to his physical infirmity. Certainly his own health may have made him especially aware of the brevity of life. But he believed that, in light of eternity, life on earth was short for everyone—even children. His poem "Children Called to Christ" reflects this understanding:

> Like mist on the mountain,
> Like ships on the sea,
> So swiftly the years
> Of our pilgrimmage flee;
> In the grave of our fathers
> How soon we shall lie!
> Dear children, to-day
> To a Saviour fly.[4]

M'Cheyne's clear view of eternity provided motivation for a life of holiness. In his understanding, sin was not only offensive

---

2. David Victor Yeaworth, "Robert Murray M'Cheyne (1813–1843): A Study of an Early Nineteenth-Century Scottish Evangelical" (PhD diss., Edinburgh, 1957), 124.

3. Andrew A. Bonar, *Memoir and Remains of Robert Murray M'Cheyne* (1844; repr., Edinburgh: Banner of Truth, 2004), 282–83.

4. A. Bonar, *Memoir and Remains*, 638.

to God—it was unwise for the believer. He believed that every sin committed by a Christian would, in some way, detract from his glory in eternity. In a letter to someone identified only as E. R., he wrote, "Remember that it is our happiness to be under grace, and every sin will be bitterness in the end, and will take something out of your eternal portion of glory."[5] M'Cheyne made this same point strongly in a sermon entitled "Follow the Lord Fully":

> Every man shall be rewarded according as his work has been. Some will be made rulers over five, some over ten cities. I have no doubt that every sin, inconsistency, backsliding and decay of God's children takes away something from their eternal glory. It is a loss for all eternity; and the more fully and unreservedly we follow the Lord Jesus now, the more abundant will our entrance be into his everlasting kingdom. The closer we walk with Christ now, the closer will we walk with him to all eternity.[6]

M'Cheyne's clear views of the reality of eternal things caused him to hold material wealth loosely. In a sermon on the Song of Solomon, he said, "An experienced Christian looks upon everything here as not abiding; for the things that are seen are temporal, but the things that are not seen are eternal."[7] M'Cheyne knew that the love of money could be an idol that could detract from one's love for God. In a message on Hosea 14:8 ("What Have I to Do Anymore with Idols?"), he said, "I believe they are happiest who are living only for eternity, who have no object in the world to divert their hearts from Christ.... Dear souls, if you have felt the love of God—the dew—you must dash down this idol. You must not love money. You must be more open-hearted, more open-handed, *to the poor*."[8]

---

5. A. Bonar, *Memoir and Remains*, 309.

6. Robert Murray M'Cheyne, *From the Preacher's Heart* (1846; repr., Geanies House, Scotland: Christian Focus, 1993), 382.

7. A. Bonar, *Memoir and Remains*, 383.

8. A. Bonar, *Memoir and Remains*, 506–7.

M'Cheyne apparently practiced what he preached in regard to material things. David Yeaworth provides us with a note written in M'Cheyne's Bible next to Luke 12:22 ("do not worry about your life"). The note reads, "How sweet is a holy carelessness about these things." Yeaworth further notes that M'Cheyne's parents were fairly well-to-do, and on one occasion his mother offered him some chairs worth twenty-seven shillings apiece and a French bed for his manse. M'Cheyne declined the gift as too costly and unnecessary.[9]

Like Jonathan Edwards before him, M'Cheyne believed that heaven was a "world of love."[10] He longed to experience the love and joy of heaven, and this longing gave shape to his ministry. M'Cheyne preached a message titled "Blessed Are the Dead," in which he explained the benefits of the life to come for the believer. Concerning the coming liberty from sin and its consequences, he said, "Oh, let this make you willing to depart, and make death look pleasant, and heaven a home…. It is the world of holy love, where we shall give free, full, unfettered, unwearied expression to our love forever."[11]

For M'Cheyne, a Christian's death was a doorway into a life of joy in the presence of the Lord. As he wrote to a friend: "A few more trials, a few more tears, a few more days of darkness, and we shall be for ever with the Lord!… All dark things shall yet be cleared up, all sufferings healed, all blanks supplied, and we shall find fullness of joy (not one drop wanting) in the smile and presence of our God."[12]

As a pastor, M'Cheyne encountered death often. In his tract titled "Reasons Why Children Should Fly to Christ without Delay," he noted that more than half of the people in Glasgow died before the age of twenty.[13] He was regularly called upon to

---

9. Yeaworth, "Robert Murray M'Cheyne," 135.

10. Jonathan Edwards, *Heaven: A World of Love* (Edinburgh: Banner of Truth, 2008).

11. A. Bonar, *Memoir and Remains*, 502.

12. A. Bonar, *Memoir and Remains*, 333.

13. A. Bonar, *Memoir and Remains*, 586.

conduct funerals for those in his large parish. When those who had died were followers of Jesus, M'Cheyne could offer the family and friends great hope in light of the life to come. On one occasion, he used his poetic skill to give comfort to a grieving family. The closing lines of the poem read:

> The precious dust beneath that lies,
> Shall at the call of Jesus rise,
> To meet the Bridegroom in the skies,
> That day we'll meet again.[14]

M'Cheyne's all-surpassing fellowship with the everlasting God made him especially aware of eternal things. Heaven and hell were more real to him than to most Christians. He was able to set his affections on things above (Col. 3:2) and to speak with authority about eternal realities. As he wrote to his sister, Eliza, while he was traveling through France, "Ah, dear Eliza, every step I take, and every new country I see, makes me feel more that there is nothing real, nothing true, but what is everlasting."[15]

Boldness and Passion for Evangelism

> To keep close to Christ in secret, having near communion with God; there is nothing can give boldness like that.
>
> —ROBERT MURRAY M'CHEYNE,
> *The Seven Churches of Asia*

M'Cheyne's private devotional life not only gave him awareness of eternal realities, it also resulted in power for his public ministry of evangelism. Quiet time in fellowship with God emboldened him and gave him compassion for those without Christ. For him, evangelism was not a duty but a passion. He felt there was no greater work than evangelism, for "one soul is worth all the

---

14. A. Bonar, *Memoir and Remains*, 647–48.

15. Robert M. M'Cheyne, *Familiar Letters by the Rev. Robert Murray M'Cheyne* (1848; repr., Charleston, S.C.: Bibliolife, 2009), 34.

material universe; for when the sun grows dim with age, that soul will still live."[16]

M'Cheyne knew that souls were eternal and would live forever in either heaven or hell. This awareness, joined with his compassion, compelled him to speak clearly and often about the danger of hell. To those who felt it was harsh to speak of hell, he said:

> Sometimes you say, "Why are you so harsh?" O poor soul! It is because the house is on fire. Oh then, can we speak too harshly?–Can we knock too loudly at the door of your consciences?
>
> I remember what a woman once told John Newton on her deathbed: she said, "You often spoke to me of Christ; but Oh! You did not tell me enough about my danger." Oh! I fear many of you will tell me the same. Oh! I fear many may reproach me on a deathbed, or in hell, that I did not tell you oftener that there was a hell. Would to God I had none to reproach me at last! God help me to speak to you plainly![17]

For all of his urgency, M'Cheyne was able to speak with gentleness born of genuine love for his hearers. He urged all Christians to speak gently to those without Christ: "Be gentle to them that are where you were. Oh! It ill becomes you to be proud and bitter over others—when you were in the same case yesterday. Rather pray for them—and weep for them—and say with the lamb-like gentleness of Christ: 'Neither do I condemn thee; go and sin no more.'"[18]

M'Cheyne believed that ministers, especially, must be passionate about evangelism. During the ordination sermon for the Rev. P. L. Miller, M'Cheyne said:

> If a neighbor's house were on fire, would we not cry aloud and use every exertion? If a friend were drowning, would we be ashamed to strain every nerve to save him? But alas!

---

16. Robert M. M'Cheyne, *A Basket of Fragments* (1848; repr., Geanies House, Scotland: Christian Focus, 2001), 108.

17. M'Cheyne, *A Basket of Fragments*, 142.

18. Yeaworth, "Robert Murray M'Cheyne," 221.

The souls of our neighbors are even now on their way to everlasting burnings,—they are ready to be drowned in the depths of perdition. Oh, shall we be less earnest to save their never-dying souls, than we would to save their bodies? How anxious was the Lord Jesus in this! When He came near and beheld the city, He wept over it. How earnest was Paul! "Remember that by the space of three years I ceased not to warn everyone night and day with tears." Such was George Whitfield; that great man scarcely ever preached without being melted into tears. Brethren, there is need of the same urgency now.[19]

M'Cheyne was troubled by ministers who "handle the Word of God deceitfully," failing to warn the unconverted by "stroking their consciences with feathers dipped in oil instead of piercing them with the Sword of the Spirit." To those who were bothered by his urgency, he said, "You will not thank us in eternity for rocking your cradle and lulling you asleep over the pit of hell."[20]

M'Cheyne's boldness and passion for evangelism were also seen outside the pulpit, as his zeal to reach others was often apparent in personal witnessing. He once said, "I think I can say I have never risen a morning without thinking how I could bring more souls to Christ."[21] William Burns records in his diary a memorable story about M'Cheyne's readiness for personal evangelism. He shares the story as he learned it from "Jean D.," the mother of a young man who had begun attending St. Peter's. Burns writes:

One of her sons now comes regularly to St. Peter's from Longforgan, a distance of five miles. The origin of this is very remarkable. One day in winter, he and another man were working in a quarry, and happened to be beside a fire, when a person came up on a pony and, for what reason they did not know, came off, and went up to them. He entered

19. A. Bonar, *Memoir and Remains*, 404.
20. Yeaworth, "Robert Murray M'Cheyne," 194.
21. Marcus L. Loane, *They Were Pilgrims* (Edinburgh: Banner of Truth, 2006), 1,150.

into conversation on the state of their souls, drawing some alarming truths from the blazing fire. The men were surprised, and said, "Ye're nae common man." "Oh yes," says he, "just a common man." One of the men recognized him as Mr. M'Cheyne, and they were so much impressed that Jean D.'s son resolved, as soon as the weather would allow, to come in to hear him. The consequence has been, that he has continued to come regularly. She hopes that he is really a converted man, and told me that he has been for some time a member of a prayer-meeting. What a striking lesson to be "instant in season and out of season."[22]

Even the *Dundee Warder*, a local paper, noted M'Cheyne's passion to turn every opportunity to write into a presentation of the gospel: "Every note from his hand had a lasting interest about it; for his mind was so full of Christ, that, even in writing about some of the most ordinary affairs, he contrived, by some natural turn, to introduce the glorious subject that was always uppermost with him."[23]

M'Cheyne somehow found time to write letters to inquirers or people who needed an understanding of the gospel. Some of these letters are detailed and lengthy and include strong appeals to turn in faith to Christ. One such letter begins simply, "My Dear G.," and includes these words:

I can assure you, from all that ever I have felt of it, the pleasures of being forgiven are as superior to the pleasures of an unforgiven man, as heaven is higher than hell. The peace of being forgiven reminds me of the calm, blue sky, which no earthly clamours can disturb. It lightens all labour, sweetens every morsel of bread, and makes a sick-bed all soft and downy; yea, it takes away the scowl of death. Now, forgiveness may be yours *now*. It is not given to those who are good.

---

22. Michael D. McMullen, *God's Polished Arrow: William Chalmers Burns* (Geanies House, Scotland: Christian Focus, 2000), 143–44.

23. Derek Prime, *Travel with Robert Murray M'Cheyne* (Leominster, England: Day One Publications, 2007), 118–19.

It is not given to any because they are less wicked than others. It is given *only* to those who, feeling that their sins have brought a curse on them which they cannot lift off, look unto Jesus, as bearing all away.[24]

But M'Cheyne was not simply called as an evangelist; he was a pastor, and he urged his church to join him in the work of evangelism. In a sermon given on July 15, 1842, he said, "But, O beloved! Think of hell! Have you no unconverted friends, who are treasuring up wrath against the day of wrath? Oh, have you no prayerless parent, no sister, nor brother? Oh, have you no compassion for them—no mercy's voice to warn them?"[25] While away from his church recuperating, M'Cheyne wrote a letter to the congregation in which he urged them to have "heart-consuming love to Jesus and the souls of men." His letter begins with a remarkable story about two Moravian missionaries and their love for souls, and he hoped the story would fuel a greater passion for evangelism in his members. He wrote:

> The most striking example of self-devotedness in the cause of Christ of which I ever heard in these days of deadness was told here last week by an English minister. It has never been printed, and therefore I will relate it to you to stir up our cold hearts, that we may give our own selves unto the Lord.
>
> The awful disease of leprosy still exists in Africa. Whether it be the very same leprosy as that mentioned in the Bible I do not know; but it is regarded as perfectly *incurable*, and so infectious that no one dares to come near. In the South of Africa there is a large Lazar-house for lepers. It is an immense space inclosed by a very high wall, and containing fields which the lepers cultivate. There is only one entrance, which is strictly guarded. Whenever any one is found with the marks of leprosy upon him, he is brought to this gate and obliged to enter in, never to return. No one is ever allowed to come out again. Within this abode of misery there are

---

24. A. Bonar, *Memoir and Remains*, 47–49.
25. M'Cheyne, *A Basket of Fragments*, 240.

multitudes of lepers in all stages of the disease. Dr. Halbeck, a missionary of the Church of England, from the top of a neighboring hill saw them at work. He particularly noticed two sowing peas in the field. The one had no hands, the other had no feet, these members being wasted away by disease. The one who lacked hands was carrying the other who lacked feet upon his back. And he again carried in his hands the bag of seed and dropped a pea every now and then, while the other pressed it into the ground with his foot. And so they managed the work of one man between the two. Ah, how little we know of the misery that is in the world!

Such is the prison-house of disease. But you will ask, who cares for the souls of the hapless inmates? Who will venture to enter in at that dreadful gate, never to return again? Who will forsake father and mother and houses and lands to carry the message of a Saviour to these poor lepers?

Two Moravian Missionaries, impelled by divine love for souls, have chosen the Lazar-house as their field of labor. They entered in, never to come out again. And I am told that as soon as these die, other Moravians are quite ready to fill up their place. Ah! My dear friends, may we not blush and be ashamed before God, that we—redeemed and with the same blood and taught by the same Spirit—should yet be so unlike these men in vehement, heart-consuming love to Jesus and the souls of men?[26]

M'Cheyne's own heart-consuming love for Christ had been shaped by his communion with the Lord. The result was an eternal perspective that gave boldness to his evangelism. As his friend and biographer, Andrew Bonar, wrote of him, "Two things he seems never to have ceased from,—the cultivation of personal holiness, and the most anxious effort to save souls."[27]

---

26. Robert Murray M'Cheyne, *Pastoral Letters* (1844; repr., Shoals, Ind.: Kingsley, 2003), 53–55.

27. A. Bonar, *Memoir and Remains*, 149.

Chapter 10

———— ❧ ————

Communion with
the Holy Spirit

Thus you see how Mr. M'Cheyne's life of prayer
and holiness gave him power, so that his words are
taking effect in the hearts and lives of his hearers
to this day.

—J. C. SMITH, *Robert Murray M'Cheyne:*
A Good Minister of Jesus Christ

A notable result of Robert Murray M'Cheyne's close communion
with God was the power of the Holy Spirit that was evident in his
life. In July 1844, the *Presbyterian Review* said of him, "His ministry at Dundee was a constant awakening…a demonstration of
the Spirit accompanied his presence."[1] M'Cheyne longed for the
power of the Spirit in his life and always felt in need of more.
His first sermon preached at St. Peter's was from Isaiah 61:1–3
("The Spirit of the Lord GOD is upon Me, because the LORD has
anointed Me"). When he spoke from this passage on his six-year
anniversary at the church, he proclaimed, "The more anointing
of the Holy Spirit, the more success will the minister have." Yet,
M'Cheyne lamented his own lack of this anointing, saying in the
same message, "In looking back upon my ministry, I am persuaded

———————

1. David Victor Yeaworth, "Robert Murray M'Cheyne (1813–1843): A
Study of an Early Nineteenth-Century Scottish Evangelical" (PhD diss., Edinburgh, 1957), 206.

that this has been the great thing wanting. We have not been like the green olive-trees; we have not been like John the Baptist, filled with the Holy Ghost."[2]

Though others felt the power of the Spirit in his life was very evident, M'Cheyne did not. To his friend Andrew Bonar, he wrote, "But, oh, I need much the living Spirit to my own soul! I want my life to be hid with Christ in God. At present there is too much hurry, and bustle, and outward working, to allow the calm working of the Spirit on the heart. I seldom get time to meditate, like Isaac, at evening-tide, except when I am tired; but the dew comes down when all nature is at rest—when every leaf is still."[3] M'Cheyne believed that the anointing of the Holy Spirit flowed from "the calm working of the Spirit on the heart," and he believed this work of the Spirit required quiet time in God's presence. Therefore, he considered such time to be his first and most important work.

M'Cheyne also longed for the members of his church to enjoy close communion with God and the "falling dew of His Spirit." In a pastoral letter dated January 30, 1839, he wrote,

> Maintain a closer walk with God, so that when I return— as God gives me now good hope of doing—I may rejoice to see what great things God has done for your souls. God feeds the wild flowers on the lonely mountainside without the help of man, and they are as fresh and lovely as those that are daily watched over in our gardens. So God can feed His own planted ones without the help of man, by the secretly falling dew of His Spirit.[4]

Communion with the Holy Spirit

M'Cheyne frequently spoke to his church about the role of the Holy Spirit and of the "holy friendship that subsists between the Holy

---

2. Andrew A. Bonar, *Memoir and Remains of Robert Murray M'Cheyne* (1844; repr., Edinburgh: Banner of Truth, 2004), 577–78.

3. A. Bonar, *Memoir and Remains*, 63.

4. Robert Murray M'Cheyne, *Pastoral Letters* (1844; repr., Shoals, Ind.: Kingsley, 2003), 18.

Spirit and a believer's soul."[5] In one message, he spoke of the role of the Holy Spirit in this way: "He comforts you with sweet views of Christ. He lifts you up to have fellowship with the Father and the Son. You live in the Spirit and pray in the Spirit and are in the Spirit on the Lord's day." He concluded this message by saying, "Be filled with the Spirit and lean on the promise. If the Spirit dwells in you he knows the glories of the heavenly inheritance, he will lift your heart toward heaven, so that you shall say, day by day, 'Now is our salvation nearer than when we believed.'"[6] M'Cheyne was able to speak to his members about the role of the Holy Spirit with an authority born of his own experience. In one message, he said,

> Learn to hold intimate communion with God. The Spirit of God will continually be lifting the heart to sweet adoring thoughts of God.... Well, then, if God has put his Spirit within you, here is a friend more than all earth can give and, oh, he is within you. He is the Spirit of truth, ask him for light. He is the Comforter, ask for comfort. Unbosom everything to this indwelling Friend.[7]

M'Cheyne himself had learned to enjoy intimate fellowship with God, and he seemed especially aware of the need for the Spirit's empowering in everything he did. Even in his letters, he often expressed his reliance upon the Holy Spirit to use the words he was writing. In his first pastoral letter while away from St. Peter's, he wrote, "May the Holy Spirit guide the pen, that what is written may be blessed to your comfort and growth in grace."[8] His sixth pastoral letter was introduced with these words: "May this letter be blessed to you by the breathing of the Holy Spirit."[9]

---

5. Robert M. M'Cheyne, *A Basket of Fragments* (1848; repr., Geanies House, Scotland: Christian Focus, 2001), 159.

6. Robert Murray M'Cheyne, *The Passionate Preacher: Sermons of Robert Murray M'Cheyne*, ed. Michael D. McMullen (Geanies House, Scotland: Christian Focus, 1999), 212–15.

7. M'Cheyne, *The Passionate Preacher*, 72.

8. M'Cheyne, *Pastoral Letters*, 13.

9. M'Cheyne, *Pastoral Letters*, 53.

The evidence of the Spirit's power in M'Cheyne's life was perhaps most visibly manifested during the period of revival at St. Peter's. This was a time when, in his words, "I have myself frequently seen the preaching of the word attended with so much power, and eternal things brought so near, that the feelings of the people could not be restrained."[10] As the Spirit drew the people, M'Cheyne was almost overwhelmed by the number of inquirers during this time. He noted twenty conversions in one evening and four hundred visits by inquirers during the first months of the revival. M'Cheyne regarded all of this as "a very delightful but laborious duty."[11] When the Spirit comes in power, He keeps His servants busy!

Humility and the Spirit's Power

M'Cheyne held a thoroughly biblical and orthodox understanding of the person and work of the Holy Spirit. He believed that the Spirit was God, the Third Person of the Trinity. In a message on "The Work of the Spirit in the Heart," he said, "The believer has God as an abiding guest, whether he is at rest or walks by the wayside. God dwells in him and walks in him. So the Spirit is not like a well of water to which the believer may go to draw the refreshing water of life, but the Spirit is in him, a well of water, springing up."[12] While M'Cheyne's doctrine of the Holy Spirit was the same as that of all Reformed Christians, his practice was not. He displayed a longing—a hunger and thirst—for the Spirit's power that far surpasses that of the average minister. Perhaps one explanation for this longing is that he was acutely aware of his own weakness. His physical frailty may have made him more aware of his need for God's power. In the words of one of M'Cheyne's elders at St. Peter's, "To know our *weakness* is a great secret of our power."[13]

---

10. A. Bonar, *Memoir and Remains*, 547–48.

11. Yeaworth, "Robert Murray M'Cheyne," 203.

12. Robert Murray M'Cheyne, *New Testament Sermons*, ed. Michael D. McMullen (Edinburgh: Banner of Truth, 2004), 109.

13. Kirkwood Hewat, *M'Cheyne from the Pew: Being Extracts from the Diary of William Lamb* (London: S. W. Partridge, n.d.), 111.

Dr. David Robertson is the current pastor at St. Peter's Church in Dundee, the same church where M'Cheyne served as pastor. In his book *Awakening: The Life and Ministry of Robert Murray M'Cheyne*, he notes that M'Cheyne would have abhorred the tendency that some have had to regard him as a "Protestant Saint." Robertson writes of M'Cheyne, "He often lamented of his 'coldness' and how he had preached himself and not the Saviour. And he was not lying. Or being falsely humble. He was all too aware of his own weaknesses and the danger of religious hypocrisy—where others build you up as an example and you are tempted to believe and live their expectations." Robertson goes on to note the encouragement provided by M'Cheyne's example: "Getting to know McCheyne and his work has been a most thrilling and humbling experience. But the greatest thing of all is this—latterly my thoughts have been drawn less and less to McCheyne and more and more on the sheer glory, wonder, grace and love of Jesus Christ. That is of course what McCheyne would have wanted."[14]

M'Cheyne's humility and desire that God alone receive glory is especially seen in his letters to other ministers. To Rev. Dan Edwards, he wrote,

It is our truest happiness to live entirely for the glory of Christ,—to separate between "I" and "the glory of Christ." We are always saying, "What have *I* done?—Was it *my* preaching—*my* sermon—*my* influence?" whereas we should be asking, "What hath God wrought?" Strange mixed beings we are! How sweet it will be to drop our old man, and be pure as Christ is pure![15]

In a letter to Rev. P. L. Miller, M'Cheyne wrote, "Lie low in self, and set both feet on the Rock of Ages."[16] And to W. C. Burns,

14. David Robertson, *Awakening: The Life and Ministry of Robert Murray M'Cheyne* (Geanies House, Scotland: Christian Focus, 2010), 219–20.
15. A. Bonar, *Memoir and Remains*, 282.
16. A. Bonar, *Memoir and Remains*, 323.

M'Cheyne included a word of caution when he wrote to celebrate the revivals at Kilsyth and Dundee:

> The work at Kilsyth seems to be owned by all God's true servants as not the work of man, but indeed divine. What a great joy to you and to your excellent father to have your labour thus honored of God! The Lord preserve you both from the personal danger to your own souls which such success exposes you to![17]

Burns apparently welcomed such advice from M'Cheyne and shared his friend's desire to remain humble and give all glory to God alone. In a letter to M'Cheyne dated July 11, 1840, Burns wrote, "I have indeed need of much grace to keep me standing, and much more to keep me fighting at present, and I have been led to think that I will not be much blessed in the Lord's work again, until he has abased me in my own sight, and taught me, if not the people also to whom I preach in his holy name, that I am indeed all vile, and that all the glory is his alone."[18] It is apparent in both William Burns and Robert M'Cheyne that high views of God brought humble views of themselves. Both men knew that while God opposes the proud, He gives His grace to the humble (James 4:6).

But another reason for M'Cheyne's great thirst for the Spirit's power was the closeness of his daily communion with Christ. The "holy friendship" with the Spirit that he taught was not a mere theory for him. He seemed to have an understanding of "the communion of the Holy Spirit" (2 Cor. 13:14) that few others have had. The closing words to his sermon "Grieve Not the Spirit" attest to this:

> I would say *to those who are receiving the refreshing gales of the Spirit*, grieve him not; walk softly with this friend. When he draws, run after him. Above all, follow his warnings. When

---

17. A. Bonar, *Memoir and Remains*, 273.

18. Michael D. McMullen, *God's Polished Arrow: William Chalmers Burns* (Geanies House, Scotland: Christian Focus, 2000), 269.

he says, Do not go with this companion, go not with him. When he says, Go not into that path, go not. "Thou shalt hear a voice behind thee saying, This is the way, walk ye in it, when ye turn to the right hand, and when ye turn to the left." Happy souls that grieve not the Holy Spirit. Soon he shall fill that soul, and leave nothing in it but himself. Soon we shall be like him, for we shall see him as he is. Amen.[19]

Communion with God was not an obligation for M'Cheyne. It was a passion. He believed that fellowship with his Lord was a gift, and one to be cherished. In expressing his desire to be as close as possible to Christ, M'Cheyne reflected upon the disciples. He noted that all were with Christ, but three—Peter, James, and John—were especially close. These were the three taken with Jesus to the Mount of Transfiguration, and M'Cheyne saw in them a model for his life, and for ours. He said, "In the Church of Christ there are some who are not only of the twelve, but of the three— men who are not only believers, but eminent believers—men who are specially near to God. It is good to be among the twelve, but better to be among the three. *Covet earnestly the best gifts.*"[20]

During his brief ministry, M'Cheyne walked with God in a way that was exceptional. Many people were moved by the humility and holiness that flowed from his life of prayer. His close communion with Christ gave him a clear view of eternal realities. His fellowship with God resulted in boldness and passion for evangelism. The power of the Holy Spirit was evident in his life.

So what can we learn from M'Cheyne's exceptional communion with God? What principles can we observe from his devotional life that we can apply to our own? Those are the questions to which we will now turn.

---

19. M'Cheyne, *A Basket of Fragments*, 166.
20. Hewat, *M'Cheyne from the Pew*, 60–61.

PART 3
Learning from M'Cheyne

Chapter 11

———— ❧ ————

Really Understanding
the Gospel

> *For all have sinned and fall short of the glory of God,*
> *being justified freely by His grace through the redemption*
> *that is in Christ Jesus.*
> —ROMANS 3:23–24

One of the greatest lessons to be learned from Robert Murray M'Cheyne's fellowship with God is the importance of thoroughly understanding the gospel. His grasp of this message revealed in Scripture shaped his understanding of the person of God and ignited his love for Christ. In the gospel, he saw the infinite holiness of God contrasted with human sin. He also saw the love of God poured out in Christ to reconcile sinful humans to himself. He lived his brief life with immense gratitude for this love.

M'Cheyne's understanding of the gospel is revealed in numerous sermons and letters. But it may be most beautifully revealed in his poetry. His poem "I Am Debtor" is a blending of rich theology with personal gratitude and love for God. Consider the sixth stanza:

> Chosen not for good in me;
> Wakened up from wrath to flee,
> Hidden in the Saviour's side,
> By the Spirit sanctified,

> Teach me, Lord, on earth, to show,
> By my love, how much I owe.[1]

Here in one stanza we see M'Cheyne's understanding of several key theological concepts:

- God's graciousness in choosing the redeemed (line 1).
- God's holy wrath toward sin (line 2).
- God's work in drawing us to Himself (line 2).
- Salvation in Jesus Christ (line 3).
- Sanctification by the Holy Spirit (line 4).
- The believer's appropriate response of gratitude and love (lines 5 and 6).

This rich understanding of key elements of the gospel laid the foundation for M'Cheyne's communion with God. He understood that we should be in awe of God's holiness and yet have great personal love for Him in response to His mercy. M'Cheyne expressed this in one of his sermons when he said, "The temper of love and the temper of awful reverence meet and blend together in the believer's bosom, to form the one majestic stream of holy fear, flowing toward the Lord our God."[2] In other words, a deeper understanding of the gospel should lead us to a deeper reverence for God and a deeper love for Him.

In similar fashion, M'Cheyne taught that a Christian's joy in relating to God sprang from a right understanding of the gospel. In his sermon "The Believer's Joy in God," M'Cheyne makes the point that "so long as we are unconverted, the Almightiness of God should be terrible to us."[3] God is infinitely holy and entirely separate from all sin. Because God is perfectly just, He is bound to maintain the just demands of His law by punishing our sin. For

---

1. Andrew A. Bonar, *Memoir and Remains of Robert Murray M'Cheyne* (1844; repr., Edinburgh: Banner of Truth, 2004), 636–37.

2. Robert Murray M'Cheyne, *Old Testament Sermons*, ed. Michael D. McMullen (Edinburgh: Banner of Truth, 2004), 174.

3. Robert Murray M'Cheyne, *The Believer's Joy* (Glasgow: Free Presbyterian Publications, 1987), 29.

this reason, according to M'Cheyne, "So long as we are unconverted, the justice of God should be terrible to us."[4]

But the believer need not shrink in terror from the justice
or almightiness of God. M'Cheyne explains in this sermon that
"we are accepted through imputed righteousness."[5] Jesus, God
the Son, fully bore our judgment on the cross. Therefore the
apostle Paul could write in Romans 3:24 that we have been "justified freely by His grace through the redemption that is in Christ
Jesus." This redemption means the righteousness of Christ is
"imputed" to the believer. God declares the believer just, forgiven,
and righteous through the work of Christ. Because God Himself
has done the work of making us accepted through Jesus, we can
know that He loves us.

M'Cheyne continued his message on "The Believer's Joy in
God" by saying, "There is something inexpressibly pleasing to a
justified mind, to know that God was all the honour of our salvation, and we have none."[6] This work of God in bringing about our
salvation assures us of God's love, and our response is to love Him
in return. God's love, M'Cheyne states, "is the sum of the reasons
why the believer joys in God—this is the oil which feeds the lamp
of his joy."[7] Understanding the gospel causes us to honor God's
holiness, to rejoice in His love, and to long for His presence. It
creates in us a longing to know Him better and to love Him more.

It has always been true of those servants of God who have
walked most closely with Him that their lives have shown a blending of holy awe and deep love for God's presence. When Moses
stood before a burning bush on holy ground, he "hid his face, for
he was afraid to look upon God" (Ex. 3:6). Yet later Moses could
say to the Lord, "If Your Presence does not go with us, do not bring
us up from here" (Ex. 33:15). King David could write, "The voice
of the LORD divides the flames of fire. The voice of the LORD

---

4. M'Cheyne, *The Believer's Joy*, 32.
5. M'Cheyne, *The Believer's Joy*, 35.
6. M'Cheyne, *The Believer's Joy*, 35.
7. M'Cheyne, *The Believer's Joy*, 34.

shakes the wilderness." (Ps. 29:7–8) But he could also write, "The
LORD is my shepherd" (Ps. 23:1). David could pen the words,

> O LORD, our Lord,
> How excellent is Your Name in all the earth,
> Who have set Your glory above the heavens. (Ps. 8:1)

Yet David could also write such personal words as these: "My soul
follows close behind You; Your right hand upholds me" (Ps. 63:8).
The apostle Paul informed the Romans that "the wrath of God is
revealed from heaven against all ungodliness and unrighteousness
of men, who suppress the truth in unrighteousness" (Rom. 1:18).
Yet he also taught them that "the love of God has been poured out
in our hearts by the Holy Spirit who was given to us" (Rom. 5:5).

We might wonder why having a high view of God's holiness
and majesty would not deter a person from longing for God's
presence. Would it not be more natural to distance ourselves from
one so awesome and powerful? The answer lies in the gospel. In
the words of Puritan author John Owen, "This is the great *discovery* of the gospel." Owen explains that "the Father, as the fountain
of the Deity" is known to humans by his wrath against sin. Yet in
the gospel, the Father is "now revealed peculiarly as love, as full
of it unto us."[8] This "*discovery* of the gospel" includes the understanding that God maintained His righteousness by allowing
Jesus, God the Son, to bear the full judgment for our sins. In the
words of pastor and author John Piper, "The wisdom of God has
ordained a way for the love of God to deliver us from the wrath of
God without compromising the justice of God."[9]

Invitation to Communion

For M'Cheyne, the gospel was not just the way to acceptance
with God, it was also an invitation to communion with God. The
heading for one of his sermon manuscripts reads, "If you are risen

---

8. John Owen, Kelly M. Kapic, and Justin Taylor, *Communion with the Triune God* (Wheaton, Ill.: Crossway, 2007), 107.

9. John Piper, *Desiring God* (Sisters, Ore.: Multnomah, 2003), 61.

with Christ, you will seek the things of Christ (Col. 3:1)." In this message, he makes the point that human beings were created for fellowship with God. He writes:

> Man was made at the first that all his affections might embrace God. Just as the seashore with its thousands of creeks and bays was made to be filled up by the ocean, so the heart of man with its thousands of clasping affections was made to be filled and satisfied with God.[10]

But this completely changed in the garden of Eden when Adam and Eve sinned against God (Gen. 2). With the entry of sin came a change in human affections. M'Cheyne continued:

> As if the creeks and bays of the seashore were to turn round and exclude the sea from their bosom, so did fallen man turn away from God and shut out God from his bosom. The affections that were made to embrace the Creator began to embrace the creatures and herein is our sin and misery summed up; we have been lovers of pleasures more than lovers of God.[11]

But the gospel changes all of this for the believer. M'Cheyne explained, "But if you be risen with Christ then your case is changed. If you be risen by the indwelling of the Holy Ghost then you cannot but seek God and set your affections on God."[12] The transforming power of the gospel brings about a change in the affections of the redeemed. The Christian is not only cleansed of sin, but also called to communion with the living God.

The Gospel Everywhere in Scripture

M'Cheyne saw the gospel and its invitation to communion with God not only in the New Testament but throughout the Bible, with countless representations of Christ and our relationship with

---

10. Robert Murray M'Cheyne, *The Passionate Preacher: Sermons of Robert Murray M'Cheyne*, ed. Michael D. McMullen (Geanies House, Scotland: Christian Focus, 1999), 208–13.

11. M'Cheyne, *The Passionate Preacher*, 213.

12. M'Cheyne, *The Passionate Preacher*, 213.

Him in the Old Testament. Speaking of the office of the priest in the Old Testament, he said, "One part of the priest's duty was to burn incense upon the golden altar. The golden altar represents Jesus, the incense, our prayers and praises."[13]

For proclaiming the gospel and calling people to communion with Christ, M'Cheyne often turned to the Song of Solomon. Many contemporary scholars understand this Old Testament book primarily as a celebration of marital love. But prior to the nineteenth century, Christian interpreters commonly understood the book as an allegory of Christ's love for the church. M'Cheyne was clearly in this group. In a message based on Song of Solomon 5:2–16, he described the text as a "beautiful transparent veil, through which every intelligent child of God may trace some of the most common experiences in the life of the believer." He went on to explain the figurative language of the narrative: "(1) The desolate bride is the believing soul. (2) The daughters of Jerusalem are fellow-believers. (3) The watchmen are ministers. (4) And the altogether lovely one is our Lord and Saviour Jesus Christ."

In applying the passage to his audience, M'Cheyne made the point that "believers often miss opportunities of communion with Christ through slothfulness." In one of his subpoints on this theme, he said, "The hour of daily devotion is a trysting hour with Christ, in which he seeks, and knocks, and speaks, and waits."[14] Before his conclusion, M'Cheyne further explained the love of "the altogether lovely one" (Christ) for "the desolate bride" (the believer) with these words: "When I have him full in my faith as a complete surety, a calm tranquility is spread over the whole inner man—the pulse of the soul has a calm and easy flow—the heart rests in a present Saviour with a healthy, placid affection. The soul is contented with him."[15]

---

13. M'Cheyne, *The Believer's Joy*, 67.

14. Robert Murray M'Cheyne, *Sermons of Robert Murray M'Cheyne* (1961; repr., Edinburgh: Banner of Truth, 2000), 60. A *tryst* is an agreement, as between two lovers, to meet.

15. M'Cheyne, *Sermons of Robert Murray M'Cheyne*, 57–63.

The Gospel Worthy of Diligent Study

The passion with which M'Cheyne preached the gospel from both New and Old Testaments was undergirded by a life of study. He spent precious years of his short life in theological training and the study of biblical languages. He would not have been among those who suggest that academic preparation for ministry necessarily leads to spiritual dryness. But he would have insisted upon biblical instruction from devoted Christian teachers.

Early in his ministry, M'Cheyne began to love the scholarly theological writings of Jonathan Edwards. Andrew Bonar writes of M'Cheyne's days in his first pastorate at Larbert: "It was here, too, that he began to study so closely the works of Jonathan Edwards,—reckoning them a mine to be wrought, and if wrought, sure to repay the toil."[16] M'Cheyne read not only Edwards, but Thomas Boston and Philip Doddridge in his studies of revival history. In a revival message entitled "A Time of Refreshing," he said, "It was so at Pentecost. First they gave their ownselves unto the Lord. It was so with Boston, and Doddridge, and Edwards, and all the holy men of old."[17] Apparently he made references to these "holy men of old" often enough that he did not even need to explain to his church who they were.

M'Cheyne's study of theology and revival history was secondary to his study of Scripture. One of his diary entries from his seminary days reads, "Hebrew class—Psalms. New beauty in the original every time I read."[18] Andrew Bonar wrote of M'Cheyne, "He could consult the Hebrew original of the Old Testament with as much ease as most of our ministers are able to consult the Greek of the New."[19] M'Cheyne's desire to understand the entirety of Scripture is revealed in his comment to a friend: "He would be a sorry student of the Bible who would not know all that God has inspired, who would not examine into the most barren

---

16. A. Bonar, *Memoir and Remains*, 35.
17. M'Cheyne, *Sermons of Robert Murray M'Cheyne*, 19.
18. A. Bonar, *Memoir and Remains*, 15.
19. A. Bonar, *Memoir and Remains*, 29.

chapters to collect the good for which they were intended."[20] His determination to find the riches in every part of the Bible is seen in the words he wrote to comfort a bereaved friend: "The Bible is like the leaves of the lemon tree—the more you bruise and wring them the sweeter the fragrance they may throw around."[21]

The Friendship of the Holy Spirit

While M'Cheyne would have stressed the importance of good theological training and deep knowledge of Scripture, he understood that those things alone do not ensure one's close communion with God. Good doctrine is important, but it is not enough. The one who would enjoy close communion with God must have the enabling and guidance of the Holy Spirit. One of his diary entries during the time of his theological education reads, "March 8.—Biblical criticism. This must not supersede heart-work. How apt it is!"[22] Andrew Bonar recalls advice written by M'Cheyne to a young student in 1840. He encouraged the young man to "get on with your studies" and to "do everything in earnest." But he added the words, "Above all, keep much in the presence of God." To another student M'Cheyne wrote, "Pray that the Holy Spirit would not only make you a believing and holy lad, but make you wise in your studies also." He added, "The smile of God calms the spirit, and the left hand of Jesus holds up the fainting head, and his Holy Spirit quickens the affection, so that even natural studies go on a million more times more easily and comfortably."[23]

M'Cheyne's understanding of the need for both good doctrine and the power of the Holy Spirit is an important lesson for the contemporary Christian church. D. A. Carson shares his observation that students and faculty at his evangelical seminary "can devote thousands of hours to the diligent study of Scripture and yet still somehow display an extraordinarily shallow knowledge of

20. A. Bonar, *Memoir and Remains*, 35.
21. James M. Gordon, *Evangelical Spirituality* (London: SPCK, 1991), 140.
22. A. Bonar, *Memoir and Remains*, 21.
23. A. Bonar, *Memoir and Remains*, 29.

God."[24] M'Cheyne spoke in even stronger terms about the danger of doctrine without a Spirit-formed love for Christ. In a message on the Laodicean church based on Revelation 3:14–22, M'Cheyne warned that a person could have a wealth of right doctrine, yet have "an unbroken unsanctified heart." He warned, "Unsanctified knowledge will be like a millstone to sink your soul."[25]

For M'Cheyne, the remedy to having "unsanctified knowledge" was love for Jesus Christ imparted to the believer by the Holy Spirit. He spoke often about the Holy Spirit, for he knew that "the love of God has been poured out in our hearts by the Holy Spirit who was given to us" (Rom. 5:5). He spoke of the "intimate friendship" that should exist between a believer and the Holy Spirit and asked, "Can there be a greater friendship than this?"[26]

M'Cheyne clearly understood the importance of our having right doctrine. But doctrine alone is not sufficient to nurture a growing love for Jesus Christ. For this we need the dynamic working of the Holy Spirit in our lives. Richard Lovelace, former professor of church history at Gordon-Conwell Theological Seminary, makes this point strongly in *Dynamics of Spiritual Life*:

> The typical relationship between believers and the Holy Spirit in today's church is too often like that between the husband and wife in a bad marriage. They live under the same roof, and the husband makes constant use of his wife's services, but he fails to communicate with her, recognize her presence and celebrate the relationship with her.
>
> What should be done to reverse this situation? We should make a deliberate effort at the outset of every day to recognize the person of the Holy Spirit, to move into the light concerning his presence in our consciousness and to open up our minds and to share all our thoughts and plans as we gaze

---

24. D. A. Carson, *A Call to Spiritual Reformation: Priorities from Paul and His Prayers* (Grand Rapids: Baker, 1992), 15.

25. M'Cheyne, *The Believer's Joy*, 45.

26. Robert Murray M'Cheyne, *A Basket of Fragments* (1848 repr., Geanies House, Scotland: Christian Focus, 2001) , 160.

by faith into the face of God. We should continue to walk throughout the day in a relationship of communication and communion with the Spirit mediated through our knowledge of the Word, relying upon every office of the Holy Spirit's role as counselor mentioned in Scripture. We should acknowledge him as the illuminator of truth and of the glory of Christ. We should look to him as teacher, guide, sanctifier, giver of assurance concerning our sonship and standing before God, helper in prayer, and as the one who directs and empowers witness.[27]

M'Cheyne's frequent references to the Holy Spirit reveal an unusual degree of familiarity with the Third Person of the Trinity. His sermons, letters, and diary entries attest to a grateful joy he felt for the Spirit's presence. The contemporary church can learn much from M'Cheyne's emphasis on the "friendship" of the Holy Spirit. A better understanding of the gospel revealed in Scripture combined with a greater reverence and regard for the Holy Spirit can help us to love God more. Then we, like M'Cheyne, can enjoy "sweet fellowship" with the triune God.

---

27. Richard F. Lovelace, *Dynamics of Spiritual Life: An Evangelical Theology of Renewal* (Downers Grove, Ill.: InterVarsity, 1979), 131.

Learning from M'Cheyne

- Memorize Romans 3:19–26 to help gain a clearer comprehension of the gospel.

- Reflect often on the love of God as revealed in the gospel.

- Daily acknowledge your need for the guidance and enabling of the Holy Spirit.

- Thank the Lord often for His presence in your life.

Chapter 12

————— ❧❧ —————

Pleasure and Power in Prayer

One of the most valuable lessons we can learn from Robert Murray M'Cheyne is that prayer is something to be enjoyed. For him, prayer was not a mere discipline or duty to be fulfilled—it was a delight to be savored. While he knew the necessity of prayer for fruitfulness in ministry, he did not see prayer as merely a means to an end. He saw prayer as the end itself, the very heart of a believer's communion with God on earth. In a message entitled "Heirs of God" he said, "A true saint prefers his God to everything else.... Half an hour spent with God, he feels worth an eternity spent with men. God is his treasure. It is to God he calls continually."[1]

The Pleasure of Prayer
In M'Cheyne's view, prayer was a way to enjoy "heavenly pleasures" while still on earth. He noted that "man was made to seek pleasure. Fallen men find pleasure in earthly things." But he explained that the nature of a "risen soul" is to "seek heavenly pleasures."[2] In a lecture on Matthew 25:10–13, M'Cheyne taught, "The greatest joy of a believer in this world is to enjoy the presence of Christ—not

---

1. Robert Murray M'Cheyne, *The Passionate Preacher: Sermons of Robert Murray M'Cheyne*, ed. Michael D. McMullen (Geanies House, Scotland: Christian Focus, 1999), 194.
2. M'Cheyne, *The Passionate Preacher*, 214–15.

seen, not felt, not heard, but still real—the real presence of the unseen Saviour. It is this makes secret prayer sweet."[3]

Aided by the Holy Spirit, he learned that prayer was a privileged means of enjoying God's presence. His longing for prayer sprang from his longing for communion with God.

Prayer and God's Power

Another lesson to be learned from M'Cheyne is that God's power is often seen in the lives of those who pray. He himself believed this to be true, and he looked to the life of Jesus for proof. In one of his lectures, he said of Christ, "Many a time when Jesus rose a great while before day, and went up into some of the deep ravines of the mountains around, he obtained showers of the Spirit, which came down at evening as he taught the people out of the boat on the lake."[4]

It was this longing for the anointing of the Holy Spirit that led M'Cheyne to diligence in both study and prayer, but especially prayer. Andrew Bonar recalled his friend's longing for the Spirit's power when he asked M'Cheyne about his preparation for preaching. "Being asked his view of diligent preparation for the pulpit, he reminded us of Ex. xxvii. 20: *'Beaten oil—beaten oil for the lamps of the sanctuary.'* And yet his prayerfulness was greater still. Indeed he could not neglect fellowship with God before entering the sanctuary. He needed to be bathed in the love of God."[5] For this reason, M'Cheyne believed that "a minister's duty is not so much public as private" and maintained that "if a minister is to thrive in his own soul, and be successful in his work, he must be the half of his time on his knees."[6]

---

3. Robert Murray M'Cheyne, *From the Preacher's Heart* (1846; repr., Geanies House, Scotland: Christian Focus, 1993), 466.

4. M'Cheyne, *From the Preacher's Heart*, 530.

5. Andrew A. Bonar, *Memoir and Remains of Robert Murray M'Cheyne* (1844; repr., Edinburgh: Banner of Truth, 2004), 52.

6. Robert M. M'Cheyne, *A Basket of Fragments* (1848; repr., Geanies House, Scotland: Christian Focus, 2001), 187.

But the Spirit's presence and power are not needed merely for public preaching and praying; his holy influence and enabling grace are needed in all of life. M'Cheyne held that a believer's prayers could bring a holy influence to the home and have an effect on the spiritual well-being of others. In a message titled "The Quarrel between Abraham and Lot," M'Cheyne noted the unwise choice that Lot made when he left Abraham's presence. Lot failed to consider "what it was to have Abraham's prayers and council." He "forgot Abraham's tent, he forgot Abraham's altar, he forgot Abraham's morning and evening prayers." Emphasizing the benefit of the influence of a believer's prayers, M'Cheyne asked, "What is there in it to make up for a believer's prayers?"[7]

Intercessory Prayer

M'Cheyne's example reminds us of the vital importance of intercessory prayer in the life of a leader. St. Peter's was a large church of approximately a thousand members. Yet he did not relegate the ministry of praying for the needs of the congregation to others. He believed intercessory prayer should be a primary component of his ministry. When health issues forced him to abandon other pastoral duties, he continued his ministry of prayer for the members of St. Peter's. In a letter sent to the church, he told them, "The walls of my chamber can bear witness how often the silent watches of the night have been filled up with entreaties to the Lord for you all."[8] He wanted the members of St. Peter's to imitate him in this ministry of praying for others, and in a message to the church, he said, "Learn from this, my Christian friends, to beseech Jesus for your friends. Ah! Do not weary in this. He will be inquired of to do this thing. Carry your friends on your heart to Jesus."[9]

7. M'Cheyne, *Basket of Fragments*, 138–39.

8. Robert Murray M'Cheyne, *Pastoral Letters* (1844; repr., Shoals, Ind.: Kingsley, 2003), 13.

9. Robert Murray M'Cheyne, *New Testament Sermons*, ed. Michael D. McMullen (Edinburgh: Banner of Truth, 2004), 45.

On another occasion he said to his church, "Who knows how many souls would be saved if you would make serious use of daily weeping and praying before God over your unconverted friends and over the unconverted world." He reminded his hearers that King David pleaded tearfully with the Lord for those who did not keep his holy law (Ps. 119:136), pointed to the example of Paul as an intercessor for the Ephesians (Acts 20:31), and noted that Christ wept over Jerusalem (Luke 19:41). M'Cheyne concluded the message by exhorting his flock to "be like David! Be like Paul! Be like Christ in this."[10]

In a message entitled "Strong Crying and Tears," M'Cheyne focused on the ministry of Christ in prayer and applied the message to ministers, parents, and even teachers, exhorting all to pray for those in their respective spheres of influence. The example of Jesus as intercessor, he explained, shows us "the way *ministers* should pray for their flocks…the way *fathers and mothers* should pray for their children…the way *teachers* should pray for their scholars… and the way you should pray *for enemies*."[11]

How to Pray
In his "Reformation in Secret Prayer," M'Cheyne reminded himself "not to omit any of the parts of prayer—confession, adoration, thanksgiving, petition, and intercession." He especially noted his tendency to neglect worship in his regular prayer times. He wrote, "There is a constant tendency to omit *adoration*, when I forget to whom I am speaking—when I rush heedlessly into the presence of Jehovah, without remembering His awful name and character— when I have little eyesight for His glory and little admiration of His wonders."[12]

M'Cheyne gave much emphasis to the confession of sin in his times of prayer. His "Reformation" notes, "The seeds of all sins are

10. M'Cheyne, *Old Testament Sermons*, 121–22.
11. Robert Murray M'Cheyne, *Sermons on Hebrews*, ed. Michael D. McMullen (Edinburgh: Banner of Truth, 2004), 72–79.
12. A. Bonar, *Memoir and Remains*, 156.

in my heart, and perhaps all the more dangerously that I do not see them." He saw the solution to the danger of self-deception being to "pray and labour for the deepest sense of my utter weakness and helplessness that ever a sinner was brought to feel." But he did not leave himself with a sense of hopelessness regarding his own sin. His "Reformation" includes these words: "But the main defence is casting myself into the arms of Christ like a helpless child, and beseeching Him to fill me with the Holy Spirit. 'This is the victory that overcometh the world, even our faith' (1 John v. 4, 5)."[13]

M'Cheyne's commitment to intercessory prayer has been noted, but his discipline in this component of his prayer life is remarkable. His "Reformation" includes an extensive list of those about whom he felt he "ought daily to intercede." The list of more than twenty-five groups includes his relatives, friends, the Church of Scotland, vacant congregations, students of divinity, and missionaries. About this group, M'Cheyne wrote, "I ought to intercede at large for the above on Saturday morning and evening from seven to eight." Then, apparently realizing he had taken on more than he could pray for in two hours, he revised his plan. His "Reformation" continues, "Perhaps also I might take different parts for different days; only I ought daily to plead for my family and flock."[14]

The organization we see in M'Cheyne's categories for prayer points to the value of having a plan for how we will use our time in prayer. Having a plan, or pattern, for prayer helps to guard against the wandering mind. M'Cheyne noted this when he wrote, "I ought not to give up the good old habit of prayer before going to bed; but guard must be kept against sleep: planning what things I am to ask is the best remedy."[15]

In addition to planned and prioritized times of prayer, M'Cheyne stressed the need for spontaneous prayer throughout

---

13. A. Bonar, *Memoir and Remains*, 153–54.
14. A. Bonar, *Memoir and Remains*, 157.
15. A. Bonar, *Memoir and Remains*, 158.

the day and lamented that he had sometimes responded to a request for him to preach without first asking counsel of God. He added, "Often I go out to visit a sick person in a hurry, without asking His blessing, which alone can make the visit of any use." His solution was to include in his "Reformation," "I ought never to do anything without prayer, and, if possible, special, secret prayer."[16]

M'Cheyne believed that prayers should be presented to God in faith. He encouraged his members to be expectant when they prayed. In one of his pastoral letters, he encouraged them to "expect answers while you are speaking in prayer! Pray and look up!"[17] In a lecture based on John 11, he said, "When we ask for something agreeable to God's will, and in the name of Christ, we know that we have the petitions which we desire of him. But the time he keeps in his own power. God is very sovereign in the time of his answers."[18] M'Cheyne balanced the union of God's sovereignty and our confidence in prayer by stressing that we should pray, as much as possible, for things that we know will honor Christ. He noted that "many lose great peace and comfort by praying only for their private concerns." He added, "Pray for the honour of Christ. Pray, 'Hallowed be Thy Name.'"[19]

Praying Scripture

In order to pray according to God's will, M'Cheyne recommended that Scripture shape our prayers. His own practice of praying Scripture can be seen in a letter he wrote to his church in 1839. The main purpose of the letter was to teach his members about prayer. It is no surprise that he concluded the letter with a prayer for them. The prayer is formed entirely from different passages of Scripture. The letter's conclusion reads:

---

16. A. Bonar, *Memoir and Remains*, 157–58.
17. M'Cheyne, *Pastoral Letters*, 39.
18. M'Cheyne, *From the Preacher's Heart*, 481.
19. M'Cheyne, *Old Testament Sermons*, 81.

Strive together in your prayers to God for me. I thank my God upon every remembrance of you, always in every prayer of mine for you all making request with joy. Now the God of patience and consolation grant you to be like-minded one toward another according to Jesus Christ. The God of hope fill you with all peace and joy in believing. And the God of peace be with you all. Amen.[20]

M'Cheyne's example reminds us that the Bible can be our greatest prayer book. The New Testament provides us with several prayers offered up by the apostle Paul, and his frequent prayers for the early Christian churches provide us with God-inspired words to pray for ourselves and others. Many of these prayers focus on the spiritual growth of those for whom he prayed (Eph. 1:16–19; 3:14–19; Phil. 1:9–11; Col. 1:9–12; 2 Thess. 1:9–12). Apparently, Paul believed that a leader's prayers for those whom he led were vital for their increased spiritual maturity.[21]

The Help of the Holy Spirit

The remarkable prayer life of M'Cheyne was not merely the result of his discipline or his great knowledge of Scripture; rather, His love for prayer was enabled and guided by the Holy Spirit. In his message "Grieve Not the Spirit," he stressed the role of the Holy Spirit in teaching us to pray. He emphasized the "intimate friendship" of the Spirit to the believer, saying, "Another friend may dwell in our neighbourhood; he may dwell in our family; but, ah! Here is a friend that dwells in us. Can there be a greater friendship than this?" This friendship, M'Cheyne explained, is exemplified

20. M'Cheyne, *Pastoral Letters*, 43. M'Cheyne's letter does not include Scripture references with this prayer. The prayer is based on several passages, including Romans 15:30; Philippians 1:3–4; and Romans 15:5.

21. An excellent resource for understanding and utilizing Paul's prayers is *A Call to Spiritual Reformation* by D. A. Carson. Carson breaks down the prayers of Paul to reveal the key emphases in his prayers for the church. He helps us to understand why Paul prayed these prayers, so we can use these biblical requests to shape our own praying.

in the Holy Spirit's role as our teacher: *"He teaches the believer to pray, yea, he prays in the believer."*[22]

One of the greatest lessons we can learn from M'Cheyne is the necessity of a moment-by-moment walk of conscious reliance upon the Holy Spirit. Christians who want close fellowship with God, effectiveness in prayer, and power in ministry must be yielded to the Spirit's control. We must recognize the arrogance and sinfulness of relying upon our own intellect and skill in ministry and live and serve others in the light of Jesus' words "without Me you can do nothing" (John 15:5). M'Cheyne and his friends Andrew Bonar, Horatius Bonar, and John Milne spoke much about the need for the church to recognize and rely upon the power of the Holy Spirit, and Horatius Bonar's biography on Milne speaks to this need. Though written in 1868, the words seem especially appropriate for the church today:

> The Church's danger ever has been to substitute a ministry of the intellect for a ministry of the Spirit; to confide in the human instead of the superhuman; and the indication that she is entangled in this snare is the feeling, conscious or unconscious, that she can do with less prayer now than formerly, on account of the progress of the age, an age which is supposed not to require the supernatural helps that other ages did.[23]

---

22. M'Cheyne, *A Basket of Fragments*, 160–61.

23. Horatius Bonar, *The Life of John Milne of Perth* (1869; repr., Edinburgh: Banner of Truth, 2010), 92.

Learning from M'Cheyne

- We learn to enjoy prayer as we grow in our understanding of the "heavenly pleasures" found in communion with God.

- God's power is most evident in the lives of those who pray much.

- There is no higher ministry for the spiritual leader than intercessory prayer.

- Have a plan for when you will pray and how you will pray.

- Turn the Bible into prayer.

- Learn the friendship of the Holy Spirit in prayer. Rely upon Him as your helper in prayer.

Chapter 13

❧

The Purposeful Pursuit of Holiness

But as He who called you is holy, you also be holy in all your conduct, because it is written, "Be holy, for I am holy."

—1 Peter 1:15–16

The quality for which Robert Murray M'Cheyne is most remembered is his holiness. Bonar's *Memoir* includes numerous references to the holiness seen in the life of his friend, and he wrote: "It was testified of him that not the words he spoke, but the *holy manner* in which he spoke, was the chief means of arresting souls."[1] Bonar also wrote, "Holiness in him was manifested, not by efforts to perform duty, but in a way so natural, that you recognized therein the easy outflowing of the indwelling Spirit."[2]

On M'Cheyne's death, a tribute to his memory was written by Rev. J. Roxburgh, who noted that his "great study was to be Christ-like" and added, "He carried with him a kind of hallowing influence into every company into which he entered."[3] Some years after M'Cheyne's death, Charles Spurgeon cited him as among the

---

1. Andrew A. Bonar, *Memoir and Remains of Robert Murray M'Cheyne* (1844; repr., Edinburgh: Banner of Truth, 2004), 71.

2. A. Bonar, *Memoir and Remains*, 94.

3. A. Bonar, *Memoir and Remains*, 169.

"best and holiest men."[4] J. C. Ryle lists him as one of the "holiest men of modern times."[5]

But M'Cheyne would not have considered himself a model of holiness and often lamented his own lack of this quality. Bonar writes, "He supposed the reason why some of the worst sinners in Dundee had come to hear him was, because his heart exhibited so much likeness to theirs."[6] One of the great lessons we can learn from M'Cheyne is that holiness is inseparably linked with humility. True holiness is always characterized by a deep sense of dependence upon the Lord, and M'Cheyne believed the only way to grow in holiness was to be aware of our complete inability to make ourselves holy. He said, "In truth, true growth in grace is to grow in a sense of our weakness and to rest all on him."[7] In one of his earliest sermons (preached in April 1835), M'Cheyne urged his hearers to "pray then that you may be so emptied of all glorifying in yourself, that you may be convinced so thoroughly not only of your own utter sinfulness but of your own utter weakness." He then called his audience to "be willing no longer to go about establishing your own holiness any more than your own righteousness."[8]

This understanding that holiness and humility are inseparable springs from a high view of the majestic holiness of God. For this reason, M'Cheyne could say that the "most eminent believers are the lowliest." He explained that the "nearer you take anything to the light, the darker its spots appear; and the nearer you live to God, the more you will see your own utter vileness."[9] His high view of God's holiness sprang from a deep knowledge of Scripture and his rich communion with the Lord; his walk with God

---

4. C. H. Spurgeon, *Lectures to My Students* (Peabody, Mass.: Hendrickson), 44.

5. J. C. Ryle, *Holiness* (Moscow, Idaho: Charles Nolan, 2001), xxi.

6. A. Bonar, *Memoir and Remains*, 65.

7. Robert Murray M'Cheyne, *The Passionate Preacher: Sermons of Robert Murray M'Cheyne*, ed. Michael D. McMullen (Geanies House, Scotland: Christian Focus, 1999), 44.

8. M'Cheyne, *The Passionate Preacher*, 160.

9. Robert Murray M'Cheyne, *From the Preacher's Heart* (1846; repr., Geanies House, Scotland: Christian Focus, 1993), 497.

led him to conclude that "holiness is the brightest attribute of Jehovah."[10] He also taught, "It is a part of the nature of God to love holiness, and to hate wickedness wherever He sees it."[11] If it is true that God loves holiness and hates wickedness, what hope do any of us have for living a life that pleases God? His answer was that God is not only our redeemer but also our sanctifier.

The Holy Spirit, the Great Sanctifier

The need for believers to live more holy lives was a frequent theme in M'Cheyne's preaching. But he did not teach his hearers that their progress in holiness depended upon themselves. The ultimate responsibility for this work—sanctification—belongs to the Holy Spirit. M'Cheyne said, "It is for this very end the Holy Ghost is given. He dwells in your bosom for no other end but to make you holy."[12]

In a message preached at St. Peter's in 1837, M'Cheyne declared that God's gift of the Spirit is the "greatest of all the privileges of a Christian" and explained that Christians could not overcome the "evil heart, the tempting world, and the devil himself" by their own power. Yet, he said, the Holy Spirit helps us: "The Spirit guides into the way of holiness."[13] In a sermon based on Romans 8:13, M'Cheyne spoke of the need to "mortify the deeds of the body" and raised the question, "How are we to do this?" He answered, "It is through the Spirit—this is the secret of gospel holiness; never forget it." He went on to speak of the "fire" of sin, saying, "The only way to put out the fire is to let in the water of the Spirit."[14]

10. Robert M. M'Cheyne, *A Basket of Fragments* (1848; repr., Geanies House, Scotland: Christian Focus, 2001), 106.

11. Robert Murray M'Cheyne, *New Testament Sermons*, ed. Michael D. McMullen (Edinburgh: Banner of Truth, 2004), 131.

12. Robert Murray M'Cheyne, *The Believer's Joy* (Glasgow: Free Presbyterian Publications, 1987), 91.

13. Robert Murray M'Cheyne, *Old Testament Sermons*, ed. Michael D. McMullen (Edinburgh: Banner of Truth, 2004), 74–75.

14. M'Cheyne, *A Basket of Fragments*, 286.

M'Cheyne taught that the Holy Spirit draws the believer to greater holiness not by fear, but by love. For a sermon entitled "The Love of Christ," his notes read, "No man was ever frightened into love, and therefore, no man was ever frightened into holiness." He went on to note that God "hath invented a way of *drawing us* to holiness. By showing us the love of his Son, he calleth forth our love." His sermon notes lead to a conclusion with these words: "And, finally, brethren, if Christ's love to us be the object which the Holy Ghost makes use of at the very first, to draw us to the service of Christ, it is by means of the same object that he draws us onwards, to persevere even unto the end."[15]

This concept that God's love motivates us to a life of greater holiness was also taught by M'Cheyne's friend, Horatius Bonar, who wrote, "Under law and its curse, a man works for self and Satan; 'under grace' he works for God. It is forgiveness that sets a man a-working for God. He does not work in order to be forgiven, but because he has been forgiven; and the consciousness of his sin being pardoned, makes him long more for its entire removal than he did before.... Forgiving love constrains him."[16]

These comments by M'Cheyne and Bonar raise the question, "Should not a believer fear to sin?" Yes. But this is a fear born of reverence and love for our holy God, not a fear that He will reject us if we stumble. If our motive in not sinning is to prevent our rejection by God, we are relying upon ourselves for salvation rather than the grace of God.

M'Cheyne's emphasis on God's love for us as the motive for a life of holiness does not mean that he disregarded the numerous warnings about sin and judgment found in Scripture. His many evangelistic messages on hell and future judgment show that he followed the biblical instruction: "but others save with fear, pulling them out of the fire, hating even the garment defiled by the

---

15. Robert Murray M'Cheyne, *Sermons of Robert Murray M'Cheyne* (1961; repr., Edinburgh: Banner of Truth, 2000), 10–11.

16. Horatius Bonar, *God's Way of Holiness* (Geanies House, Scotland: Christian Focus, 1999), 57–58.

flesh" (Jude 23). Yet M'Cheyne realized that for the believer, fear was a poor taskmaster in the work of sanctification. In the words of 1 John 4:18–19: "There is no fear in love; but perfect love casts out fear, because fear involves torment. But he who fears has not been made perfect in love. We love Him because He first loved us." Our love for God is a response to His love for us, which was revealed in the gospel. An understanding of this love is a strong motivator to live for the glory of God. M'Cheyne put it this way:

> But now I wish to show you that the Gospel does far more than restore us to the state from which we fell. If rightly and consistently embraced by us, it brings us into a state far better than Adam's. It constrains us by a far more powerful motive. Adam had not this strong love of God to man shed abroad in his heart; and, therefore, he had not this constraining power to make him live to God. But our eyes have seen this great sight.[17]

What can we learn from M'Cheyne's understanding of how the Holy Spirit works in our sanctification? His perspective is a powerful antidote to legalism—trying to earn God's favor by our own efforts. If greater love for God is the key to our progress in sanctification, we should pray for the Holy Spirit to enable us to more fully grasp this love (Eph. 3:16–19). We should devote ourselves more fully to the joy of communion with God as our creator, redeemer, and sanctifier.

Striving for Holiness

While M'Cheyne was clear about the need to rely on the Holy Spirit in order to be made holy, he was also clear about the Christian's responsibility to pursue holiness. In a letter written to his church in 1839, he told his members to "seek to be made holier every day. Pray, strive, wrestle for the Spirit to make you like God."[18]

---

17. M'Cheyne, *Sermons of Robert Murray M'Cheyne*, 9.
18. Robert Murray M'Cheyne, *Pastoral Letters* (1844; repr., Shoals, Ind.: Kingsley, 2003), 66.

This joining of God's work and our own in the process of sanctification is well explained by contemporary author Jerry Bridges. He notes that "although sanctification is the work of the Holy Spirit, it is a work in which He involves us."[19] In explaining God's role and our role in the pursuit of holiness, Bridges notes that "God's work does not make our effort unnecessary, but rather makes it effective."[20]

M'Cheyne's own effort in the active pursuit of holiness is best seen in his "Reformation." He wrote this document for the purpose of regularly examining his own heart and life, and divides it into two sections: (1) "Personal Reformation" and (2) "Reformation in Secret Prayer."[21] M'Cheyne's "Reformation" bears interesting similarity to Jonathan Edwards's "Resolutions," and it may be that M'Cheyne was following the example of the theologian whose work he so admired. In their documents, both men expressed humble reliance upon the grace of God to enable them to progress in holiness. Edwards introduced most of his commitments to more godly behavior with the word "Resolved."[22] M'Cheyne most often used the phrase, "I ought to...."[23]

M'Cheyne's "Reformation" gives much emphasis to the confession of sin. But it also articulates M'Cheyne's commitment to daily focusing on the Lord Himself. He writes, "I ought never to forget that my body is dwelt in by the third Person of the Godhead. The very thought of this should make me tremble to sin (1 Cor. vi)." He ends the first section with the words, "'Make me Christ-like in all things,' should be my constant prayer. 'Fill me with the Holy Spirit.'"[24]

---

19. Jerry Bridges, *The Discipline of Grace: God's Role and Our Role in the Pursuit of Holiness* (Colorado Springs: NavPress, 1994), 109.

20. Bridges, *The Discipline of Grace*, 133.

21. A. Bonar, *Memoir and Remains*, 150–58.

22. Jonathan Edwards, *Jonathan Edwards' Resolutions and Advice to Young Converts*, ed. Stephen J. Nichols (Phillipsburg, N.J.: P&R, 2001), 17–26.

23. A. Bonar, *Memoir and Remains*, 150–58.

24. A. Bonar, *Memoir and Remains*, 154–56.

The fact that one of two sections in M'Cheyne's document is his "Reformation in Secret Prayer" highlights his understanding of the role of prayer in sanctification. Here we see a beautiful blending of his reliance upon God and his own determination to faithfully pursue God. Perhaps this is because M'Cheyne knew so well his complete inadequacy when it came to his progress in holiness. Perhaps he had learned by experience what he taught in one of his messages: "There is nothing more deceitful than your estimate of your own strength."[25]

The Sanctifying Power of God's Word

M'Cheyne understood that only the Holy Spirit could make him holy and believed the Bible is the primary instrument the Spirit uses in this process. In a sermon based on Ephesians 5:25–27, he explained that "Jesus is the author of sanctification." He went on to say, "Learn the means of sanctification—the Word. No holiness without the Bible." He added, "Just like a mother nourishing a child, Jesus takes a soul and nourishes it with the milk of the Word."[26] In 1837, M'Cheyne gave a message at St. Peter's in which he distinguished Christ's work in salvation from His work in sanctification. His manuscript notes read: "Christ is not done with a soul when he has brought it to the forgiveness of sins. It is only then that he begins his regular visits to the soul. In the daily reading of the Word, Christ pays daily visits to sanctify the believing soul."[27]

Although M'Cheyne read the works of Jonathan Edwards, Richard Baxter, and others, he felt no book could compare with the Bible. In a message based on Psalm 119, he said, "The best of books are but sparks from the Bible, mingled with human darkness."[28] On another occasion, he spoke of the sanctifying power of the Bible with these words: "Oh, be wiser in your Bibles

---

25. A. Bonar, *Memoir and Remains*, 478–79.
26. M'Cheyne, *A Basket of Fragments*, 91.
27. M'Cheyne, *From the Preacher's Heart*, 232.
28. M'Cheyne, *The Believer's Joy*, 15.

than in the newspaper. What good will all that ever you read in the newspaper do when you are dying?"[29]

God sanctifies us by His Word. We see this in Jesus' prayer to the Father to "sanctify them by Your truth. Your word is truth" (John 17:17). But we are responsible to "desire the pure milk of the word, that you may grow thereby" (1 Peter 2:2). Our growth in holiness will be directly related to the purposeful application of our hearts and minds to God's Word.

More Holy through Hardships

In M'Cheyne's pursuit of greater holiness, he saw God's hand at work through a variety of trials and hardships. He wrote to his church to teach them that "affliction will *certainly* purify a believer." He added, "Ah, how much dross is there in every one of you dear believers, and in your pastor."[30] As heat separates dross from a precious metal, M'Cheyne believed, so can affliction be used to separate a believer from sin. This understanding led him to speak often on the "improvement of affliction," a phrase he may have borrowed from Jonathan Edwards. One of Edwards's "Resolutions" reads, "Resolved, after afflictions to inquire what I am the better for them, what good I have got by them, and what I might have got by them."[31]

M'Cheyne's sermon titled "The Right Improvement of Affliction" gives practical guidance for progressing in holiness through trials. He wrote, "God's great design in affliction is to make you forsake your sin."[32] In his message "The Quarrel between Abraham and Lot," M'Cheyne dealt specifically with "domestic trials." Concerning such conflict in families he said, "Just as the jeweller puts the gold into the crucible, not to destroy the gold, but to separate it from the dross, so trials are intended by God to separate us from all dross."[33]

---

29. M'Cheyne, *The Believer's Joy*, 95.
30. M'Cheyne, *Pastoral Letters*, 34.
31. Edwards, *Jonathan Edwards' Resolutions*, 26.
32. M'Cheyne, *Sermons of Robert Murray M'Cheyne*, 137.
33. M'Cheyne, *A Basket of Fragments*, 134.

If God uses trials to separate us from "dross," how should we respond to trials, hardships, and afflictions? The apostle James gives us practical guidance in the New Testament letter that bears his name. James tells us first to "count it all joy when you fall into various trials, knowing that the testing of your faith produces patience" (James 1:2–3). Our second response should be to pray in faith for wisdom: "If any of you lacks wisdom, let him ask of God, who gives to all liberally and without reproach, and it will be given to him" (James 1:5). In asking for wisdom, the question, Why is this happening to me? is not as valuable as, How should I respond in this situation? Third, we should remain steadfast in our devotion to God and the sanctifying work of His Spirit in our lives. "Blessed is the man who endures temptation; for when he has been approved, he will receive the crown of life which the Lord has promised to those who love Him" (James 1:12). Fourth, we should turn from any known sin and respond to God's Word with humility and obedience. "Therefore lay aside all filthiness and overflow of wickedness, and receive with meekness the implanted word, which is able to save your souls. But be doers of the word, and not hearers only, deceiving yourselves" (James 1:21–22). By turning to God's Word in our trials, we are submitting to the primary instrument that the Holy Spirit uses in our sanctification. Rather than turning away from God in discouragement, we are turning to Him in faith. We can then expect to come through our hardships with stronger faith, increased holiness, and greater love for Jesus Christ.

More Holy and More Useful

M'Cheyne strongly believed that his usefulness in God's service depended on his holiness. In a letter to W. C. Burns in 1840, he expressed his longing for revival in Scotland. He wrote, "I am also deepened in my conviction, that if we are to be instruments in such a work, we must be purified from all filthiness of the flesh and spirit. Oh, cry for personal holiness, constant nearness to God by the blood of the Lamb." Later in the letter he added, "How much more useful might we be, if we were only more free from pride, self-conceit, personal vanity, or some secret sin that our heart knows!"[34]

Burns clearly shared his friend's determination to live a holy life so as to be effective in ministry. His journal entry of July 1, 1840, reads, "I spent the day chiefly alone, seeking personal holiness, the fundamental prerequisite in order to a successful ministry."[35] Like M'Cheyne, Burns was known for his holiness of life and the impact this had on others. Their mutual friend, John Milne, wrote of Burns, "I was struck with his close walk with God, his much and earnest prayer, his habitual seriousness, the solemnizing effect which his presence seemed to have wherever he went, and his success in leading those with whom he conversed to anxious, practical, heart-searching concern about their state in God's sight.[36]

M'Cheyne and Burns embraced an understanding of holiness and usefulness that is clearly taught in Scripture. In his second letter to Timothy, the apostle Paul wrote:

> But in a great house there are not only vessels of gold and silver, but also of wood and clay, some for honor and some for dishonor. Therefore if anyone cleanses himself from the latter, he will be a vessel for honor, sanctified and useful for the Master, prepared for every good work. (2 Tim. 2:20–21)

The idea that personal holiness is a necessary qualification for Christian service is often disregarded today. Church leaders would be wise to consider the purity of a person's walk with the Lord before offering a promotion to ministry leadership. The church would also do well to recover the understanding that the holiness of our lives is related to our impact upon the world. M'Cheyne

---

34. A. Bonar, *Memoir and Remains*, 289.

35. Michael McMullen, *God's Polished Arrow: William Chalmers Burns* (Geanies House, Scotland: Christian Focus, 2000), 181.

36. Horatius Bonar, *The Life of John Milne of Perth* (1869; repr., Edinburgh: Banner of Truth, 2010), 47.

knew this well, which is why he wrote to William Burns, "I feel there are two things it is impossible to desire with sufficient ardour,—personal holiness, and the honour of Christ in the salvation of souls."[37]

37. A. Bonar, *Memoir and Remains*, 281.

Learning from M'Cheyne

- Contemplate God's holiness as revealed in passages like Isaiah 6:1–3 and Revelation 4:8–11. Pray for a greater comprehension of your complete dependence upon the Lord.

- Be intentional about the pursuit of greater holiness in your daily devotional time.

- Rely upon the Holy Spirit to make you more holy. Ask Him to give you a greater understanding of God's love for you. Pray Ephesians 3:14–19 for yourself.

- Apply your mind and heart to God's Word daily. Memorize 1 Thessalonians 4:3–7; 5:23–24; and 1 Peter 1:15–16.

- When facing adversity, ask God to teach you how to respond and to enable you to grow in holiness.

—— ❧ ——

Chapter 14

Passion and Power
for Evangelism

In Robert Murray M'Cheyne, we see that communion with God is not merely for our own comfort, contentment, or joy. Love for God overflows in love for people, especially people in need of God's salvation, and M'Cheyne's rich fellowship with God resulted in much compassion for those without God. He hints at this understanding in a letter he wrote to the Rev. P. L. Miller in 1842. He advised him, "Get much of the hidden life in your own soul; soon it will make life spread around."[1] Because of his close communion with the Lord, he could say, "I have never risen a morning without thinking how I could bring more souls to Christ."[2]

This connection between communion with Christ and effective evangelism was stressed by M'Cheyne's friend Horatius Bonar (brother of Andrew) in his book *Words to Winners of Souls.* Bonar wrote, "Our power in drawing men to Christ springs chiefly from the fullness of our personal joy in Him, and the nearness of our personal communion with Him." This communion shapes our passions and priorities and keeps us in close tune with the guidance of the Holy Spirit. Bonar adds, "A ministry of

---

1. Andrew A. Bonar, *Memoir and Remains of Robert Murray M'Cheyne* (1844; repr., Edinburgh: Banner of Truth, 2004), 323.
2. Robert Murray M'Cheyne, *A Basket of Fragments* (1848 repr., Geanies House, Scotland: Christian Focus, 2001), 125.

power must be the fruit of a holy, peaceful, loving intimacy with the Lord."[3]

Passion for Evangelism

The understanding that close communion with God leads to passion and power for evangelism was apparently embraced by a number of M'Cheyne's associates in ministry. An unidentified person who recorded much of what took place in Edinburgh in 1841 when W. C. Burns preached at St. Luke's Church for his friend A. Moody Stuart said of Burns: "Those who had the rare privilege of meeting him in private, and seeing his close walk with God, were at no loss to understand the power which attended his public ministration. With him the winning of souls was a passion; calm, but intense, consuming."[4]

M'Cheyne's close friend and biographer, Andrew Bonar, was known for his close communion with God and his passion to reach those without Christ. Iain Murray writes that a truth seen in Bonar's life was that "communion with God brings resemblance to Christ." Murray adds that "this showed in his tender, urgent concern for the unconverted."[5] Because Jesus, the Son of Man, came "to seek and to save that which was lost" (Luke 19:10), it seems reasonable that those in close fellowship with Him would share His passion to reach the lost. Andrew Bonar lived with this passion, which can be seen in a comment he made after hearing of the death of M'Cheyne, his closest friend. Bonar wrote in his diary on Saturday, March 25, 1843: "My heart is sore. It makes me feel death near myself now. Life has lost half its joys, were it not [for] the hope of saving souls."[6]

---

3. Horatius Bonar, *Words to Winners of Souls* (Phillipsburg, N.J.: P&R, 1995), 13.

4. Michael McMullen, *God's Polished Arrow: William Chalmers Burns* (Geanies House, Scotland: Christian Focus, 2000), 72.

5. Iain Murray, "Andrew Bonar and Fellowship with Christ," *The Banner of Truth*, no. 567 (December 2010): 16.

6. Marjory Bonar, *Andrew A. Bonar, D. D.—Diary and Letters* (London: Hodder and Stoughton, 1894), 101.

An important lesson from M'Cheyne, Burns, and the Bonars is that close fellowship with God results in our having more of the Lord's passion and power for reaching the lost. Time alone with Christ should result in our having more of the compassion of Christ, who, seeing the multitudes, "was moved with compassion for them, because they were weary and scattered, like sheep having no shepherd" (Matt. 9:36). It was for this reason M'Cheyne could say, "If you will come to Jesus and drink, you shall become a fountain."[7]

Evangelism as a Priority

Evangelism was at the heart of M'Cheyne's pastoral ministry. The greatest goal of his preaching and home visitation among his members was to bring each of them to faith in Jesus Christ. In a sermon for a friend's ordination, he said, "It is well to visit the sick, and well to educate children and clothe the naked. It is well to attend presbyteries. It is well to write books or read them. But here is the main thing—preach the Word." Then he added, "Woe be unto us if we preach not the gospel!" Later in the ordination service, M'Cheyne gave a charge to the congregation. To the members about to welcome their new pastor he said, "Do not trouble him about worldly matters.—His grand concern is to get your soul saved."[8]

M'Cheyne's sermons cover a remarkable variety of topics from the Old and New Testaments. They include much instruction and exhortation intended to equip believers to live holy lives. They also consistently include the proclamation of the gospel, along with a call to trust Jesus Christ alone for salvation. His preaching reveals his fundamental belief that "this is one of the chief parts of a minister's duty—to warn the unconverted."[9]

M'Cheyne did not merely evangelize through his sermons. He visited both members and nonmembers of his church in their

7. Robert Murray M'Cheyne, *From the Preacher's Heart* (1846; repr., Geanies House, Scotland: Christian Focus, 1993), 306.

8. A. Bonar, *Memoir and Remains*, 401–8.

9. M'Cheyne, *A Basket of Fragments*, 114.

homes. While his visits included pastoral prayer and care, his most urgent concern was to be assured of each person's salvation. Andrew Bonar notes that M'Cheyne often visited in the community with his object being "to get souls saved." He cites this entry from M'Cheyne's diary: "Good visiting day. Twelve families; many of them go nowhere. It is a great thing to be well furnished by meditation and prayer before setting out; it makes you a far more full and faithful witness."[10]

It is important to note that M'Cheyne served a church of a thousand or more people. Yet he still engaged in frequent personal evangelism. The contemporary church might see significant renewal if we pastors followed the example set by M'Cheyne in making evangelism a vital component of pastoral ministry.

It would be a mistake to conclude that M'Cheyne thought evangelism was solely the duty of the ordained minister. He believed that the responsibility and privilege of evangelism was for every Christian. In a message entitled "Christian Behavior," he stressed that Christians are not to live in isolation from the world. Rather, he said, "God calls His people His witnesses. They are like salt in the midst of corruption, or a dew in the desert."[11] In another message, he emphasized the need for Christians to be witnesses in their homes. He said, "A candle shines best of all in a room, and so a true heaven-lighted Christian should shine brightest in his own home.... If you can preach like Paul in the world and yet forget to teach your children and servants at home, then I stand in doubt of you."[12]

For M'Cheyne and the church he served, evangelism was a priority. This focus did not come about because evangelism was a strategy for church growth; rather, it was a result of M'Cheyne's

---

10. A. Bonar, *Memoir and Remains*, 60.

11. Robert Murray M'Cheyne, *New Testament Sermons*, ed. Michael D. McMullen (Edinburgh: Banner of Truth, 2004), 280–81.

12. Robert Murray M'Cheyne, *Old Testament Sermons*, ed. Michael D. McMullen (Edinburgh: Banner of Truth, 2004), 162.

communion with God. Time spent with God resulted in his having more of the Lord's compassion for those without Jesus.

Greater Awareness of Eternal Realities

M'Cheyne's passion for sharing the gospel was related to his keen awareness of eternity. His time spent in God's presence overflowed with a greater sense of the brevity of life on earth and enabled him to view life with an eternal perspective. For this reason, he understood the immense value of a human soul. He said, "One soul is worth all the material universe; for when the sun grows dim with age, that soul will still live."[13]

This awareness of eternal realities gave an urgency to M'Cheyne's evangelism. People must be reached with the gospel because "life is like a stream made up of human beings, pouring on, and rushing over the brink into eternity."[14] M'Cheyne felt that ministers, especially, must never be timid in presenting the gospel. He said, "If you were beside a dying man and knew that in half an hour he would be in eternity, what would you say to him? Would you not tell him of the Person and love of Jesus?"[15]

M'Cheyne often pressed his own listeners to consider the shortness of life on earth and to turn in faith to Jesus while they could. In notes for a message entitled "Time Is Short," he wrote: "The time to be spent in this world is very short; it is but an inch of time, a short half-hour. In a very little, it will all be over," and "Your years are numbered. To many this is the last year they shall ever see in this world." Concerning those who had died without Christ, M'Cheyne said, "What would they not give, brethren, for such an opportunity as you have this day?"[16]

A clear eternal perspective caused M'Cheyne to speak straightforwardly about hell. In one sermon he said, "Dear friends, I often think when I look to your houses as I pass along, and when I look

---

13. M'Cheyne, *A Basket of Fragments*, 108.
14. A. Bonar, *Memoir and Remains*, 499.
15. M'Cheyne, *New Testament Sermons*, 158.
16. M'Cheyne, *From the Preacher's Heart*, 198–205.

in your faces, that ministers are like watchmen—they see the fire, and they give the alarm. Many of you are in danger as one in a burning house."[17] This urgency to warn his hearers about hell was especially prominent in the final year of his life. He preached four messages on the topic of eternal punishment in 1842, prior to his death in March 1843. One of those messages, "Future Punishment Eternal," was based on Mark 9:44. In this message, M'Cheyne shared both Old and New Testament passages that present the doctrine of eternal punishment. He explained that King David, Jesus, and the apostle Paul all spoke clearly about a place of suffering after death for those without God's salvation. He then made the point that those with the greatest love (e.g., David, Jesus, and Paul) warned others of hell. He asked, "Do not these show you, brethren, that they that have most love in their hearts speak most of hell?" He continued, "They do not love you that do not warn you.... Oh remember that love warns!"[18]

One of the most important lessons we can learn from M'Cheyne is the importance of dealing clearly with the issue of eternity. Most of us would prefer to ignore the topic of hell, despite the fact that Jesus often warned of its reality in passages like Matthew 5:22; 13:42, 49, 50; 23:33; and 25:41. Perhaps God would be pleased to more fully empower our evangelism if we presented the fullness of His counsel when we shared the gospel.

Another lesson for us is that communion with God can give us clearer eternal perspective. Time spent with God will enable us to better see life as He sees it. A clearer view of eternity will give us a greater urgency for evangelism. Perhaps then we could say like M'Cheyne that we never rise a day without thinking about how we might be used to bring someone else to Christ.

17. Robert Murray M'Cheyne, *Sermons of Robert Murray M'Cheyne* (1961; repr., Edinburgh: Banner of Truth, 2000), 145.

18. M'Cheyne, *A Basket of Fragments*, 231–40.

The Power of the Holy Spirit for Evangelism

Despite his theological training and knowledge of Scripture, M'Cheyne knew that he was helpless to evangelize in his own strength. He understood that no Christian, regardless of intellect or training, could bring about the spiritual act of conversion in his or her own power. Evangelism must be empowered by the Holy Spirit. At the ordination service of P. L. Miller, he stressed this truth in the charge he gave to his friend: "Oh, brother, plead with God to fill you with the Spirit, that you may stand in His counsel, and cause the people to hear His words, and turn many from the evil of their ways.... Pray that you may be filled with the fire of the Holy Spirit, that you may pierce into the hard hearts of unconverted sinners."[19] In a message preached several months before his death, M'Cheyne said, "Brethren, all conversion comes from God. You might rather expect the icebergs of the Atlantic to melt without the sun than expect a sinner's heart to change without God."[20]

The humble recognition that he was helpless in ministry without God's power helped M'Cheyne to live with conscious dependence upon the Holy Spirit. This sense of dependence upon the Spirit was also characteristic of his friend W. C. Burns. In his biography of Burns, Michael McMullen writes, "Repeated journal entries testify to the fact that Burns believed that without the strength and help of the Holy Spirit, he could accomplish nothing at all. It is also clear from his *Journals*, that this became the guiding principle of his whole life and ministry."[21]

What can we learn from M'Cheyne and Burns, whose lives exhibited such dependence upon the Holy Spirit and such fruitfulness in evangelism? One lesson is that while we have an urgent responsibility to share the gospel, we ourselves can save no one. As J. I. Packer writes, "While we must always remember that it is our responsibility to proclaim salvation, we must never forget

---

19. A. Bonar, *Memoir and Remains*, 405–6.
20. M'Cheyne, *A Basket of Fragments*, 129.
21. McMullen, *God's Polished Arrow*, 29.

that it is God who saves."[22] This awareness should lead us to a conscious dependence upon the Holy Spirit. By depending upon Him, we can become less timid about our own inadequacies in sharing the gospel.

Another lesson from these leaders is the need to live our lives in the fullness of the Holy Spirit. Remarkable power attended M'Cheyne's ministry, yet he always seemed to long for more. He seemed especially aware of Jesus' words "for without Me you can do nothing" (John 15:5). And his life showed the truth of Jesus' promise that "He who abides in Me, and I in him, bears much fruit" (John 15:5).

---

22. J. I. Packer, *Evangelism and the Sovereignty of God* (Downers Grove, Ill.: InterVarsity, 1961), 27.

Learning from M'Cheyne

- Remember that our communion with God is not merely for our own benefit. Our love for God should overflow in love for people who do not yet know Him.

- Learn how to present the gospel, memorizing key verses to use in your presentation.

- Consider the many biblical passages that speak of eternal judgment for those without Christ. (Here are some verses found just in the gospel of Matthew: 5:22; 8:12; 11:23; 13:42; 13:49–50; 22:13; 23:33; 25:41; and 26:24.) Think about God's purpose in giving us so much Scripture on this subject.

- Ask God to help you to be more yielded to the control of the Holy Spirit. Pray for a greater manifestation of His power (Acts 1:8) and His fruit (Gal. 5:22–23) in your life.

Chapter 15

———— ❧•❧ ————

Passion for Revival

Robert Murray M'Cheyne's close communion with God over-flowed with vision for what God could do in his church. He regularly saw people at St. Peter's coming to faith in Jesus Christ, but he was not content with that. He longed for a sweeping work of the Holy Spirit in which great numbers of people would come to know the Lord he loved. He had read and heard of such periods of revival in the past and longed to see them in his time. In a letter written to Horatius Bonar from London, M'Cheyne reported on his own preaching while there. He wrote, "I have preached three times here; a few tears have been shed. Oh for Whitfield's week in London, when a thousand letters came! The same Jesus reigns; the same Spirit is able. Why is He restrained? Is the sin ours? Are we the bottle-stoppers of these heavenly dews?"[1]

Humility and Desire for Revival

In characteristic fashion, M'Cheyne looked first to himself in evaluating any hindrances to a greater working of the Holy Spirit in his ministry. In the same letter to Bonar, he wrote, "Oh that my soul were new moulded, and that I were effectually called a second time, and made a vessel full of the Spirit to tell only of Jesus

———————

1. Andrew A. Bonar, *Memoir and Remains of Robert Murray M'Cheyne* (1844; repr., Edinburgh: Banner of Truth, 2004), 145–46.

and His love! I fear I shall never be in this world what I desire."[2]
This humility indicated by first examining himself is found in
M'Cheyne's diary as well. One of his entries provides a record of
several people who had come to faith in Christ. M'Cheyne even
describes what he had seen as "some very evident awakenings."
Despite the encouraging things he had witnessed, he ends the
diary entry with these words: *I feel persuaded that if I could follow
the Lord more fully myself, my ministry would be used to make a deeper
impression than it has yet done.*[3]

Humble leadership in promoting revival is seen again in a
letter M'Cheyne wrote to his church prior to his departure on
the mission to the Jews. His letter expresses his great concern
over those in the church who had not yet come to Christ, caus-
ing "insupportable agony to my spirit." He then raises the issue of
"what appear to be the chief reasons why, after my two years' ministry among you, there are still so many unconverted, perishing
souls." In raising possible answers to the issue, M'Cheyne starts
with himself: *"One cause is to be sought in your minister."* He addresses
his responsibility with the words: "I do this day bewail before you
every sin in my heart and life that has kept back the light from
your poor dark souls." He adds, "Oh, you that can pray, pray that I
may come back a holy minister, a shepherd to lead the flock not by
the voice only, but to walk before them in the way of life."[4]

M'Cheyne's example reminds us that humility is an essential
quality for those who hope to experience a great working of the
Holy Spirit. Likewise, pride can be a barrier to our seeing the Spirit's
power at work. Both Old and New Testaments teach us that "God
resists the proud, but gives grace to the humble" (Prov. 3:34; James
4:6; 1 Peter 5:5). The leader who would be used by God during a
time of revival must have a vision for what God can do combined
with an understanding of his or her own utter helplessness.

---

2. A. Bonar, *Memoir and Remains*, 142.

3. A. Bonar, *Memoir and Remains*, 142.

4. Robert Murray M'Cheyne, *Pastoral Letters* (1844; repr., Shoals, Ind.:
Kingsley, 2003), 69–77.

The barrier of human pride to genuine revival was emphasized by Dr. Martyn Lloyd-Jones in his messages on revival. He stressed, "It is our arrogance, it is our pride, it is our tendency to set ourselves up and to define God after our own image, instead of falling and prostrating ourselves before him, it is that, which stands between us and these mighty blessings."[5] Humility must characterize the lives of those who hope to see God's power at work through them in revival. Humility is required because revival is, above all other things, an exalting of the glory of God. Lloyd-Jones writes, "What revival reveals above everything else is the sovereignty of God, and the iniquity, the helplessness, the hopelessness, of man in sin."[6] In revival, the sovereign God, who opposes the proud, pours His grace upon the humble.

Humble Leadership during Revival

As M'Cheyne made plans for his trip to Jewish lands in 1839, he arranged for William Burns to serve in his absence at St. Peter's. Burns was only twenty-four years old at the time and was not yet fully licensed to preach by the Church of Scotland.[7] In his reply to M'Cheyne, Burns accepted the offer while acknowledging his sense of inadequacy for the task. He wrote, "If however you still desire that I should attempt this work, I dare not refuse from any inability which the Lord who calleth me to his service is able and willing to remove."[8] This sense of personal inability combined with trust in God's faithfulness was characteristic of Burns. Michael McMullen writes, "It was Burns' own clear sense of insufficiency that actually played a major part in persuading him to accept the call to Dundee, for Burns was utterly convinced that without God he could do nothing.[9] While Burns lacked both

5. Martyn Lloyd-Jones, *Revival* (Wheaton, Ill.: Crossway, 1987), 42.

6. Lloyd-Jones, *Revival*, 42.

7. Michael McMullen, *God's Polished Arrow: William Chambers Burns* (Geanies House, Scotland: Christian Focus, 2000), 27.

8. McMullen, *God's Polished Arrow*, 28.

9. McMullen, *God's Polished Arrow*, 29.

experience and credentials, he possessed a quality that meant far more to M'Cheyne—a humble reliance upon God.

God-formed humility was vital for Burns because of the extraordinary way in which God would use him. The evidence of both gifting and power at work in his life are seen in a remarkable record made by one of the church officers at St. Peter's:

> Scarcely had Mr. Burns entered on his work in St. Peter's here, when his power as a preacher began to be felt. Gifted with a solid and vigorous understanding, possessed of a voice of vast compass and power, unsurpassed even by that of Mr. Spurgeon and withal fired with an ardour so intense and an energy so exhaustless that nothing could resist it, Mr. Burns wielded an influence over the masses whom he addressed which was almost without parallel since the days of Wesley and Whitefield.[10]

The extraordinary (and perhaps exaggerated) description of Burns by the church officer stands in stark contrast to the modest description of his ministry written by Burns himself. In a letter written to his sister soon after his arrival at St. Peter's, Burns expressed concern that the high level of spiritual maturity among some in the church might "make me to appear among them as an ignorant babbler."[11] As God worked through him at the church, Burns became especially aware of the need for God-given humility and protection from pride. A journal entry during his first month at the church reads, "Discovered through grace, an awful hungering after applause from man, and came home fearing that God may utterly forsake me in consequence of my self-seeking in his service." He goes on to express his recognition that humility expressed in prayer was vital to furthering the work God was doing: "O for a spirit of humble wrestling prayer for the outpouring of the Holy Spirit, that sinners may be awakened, and saints greatly edified and advanced."[12]

---

10. McMullen, *God's Polished Arrow*, 30.
11. McMullen, *God's Polished Arrow*, 31.
12. McMullen, *God's Polished Arrow*, 31.

Burns's longing for "a spirit of humble wrestling prayer" reminds us that an awareness of our complete dependence upon God is a foundational precursor to revival. Awareness of our dependency must be united with faith in God, who alone can bring about dramatic change in the church by pouring out His Spirit. Despite the fact that M'Cheyne and Burns were only twenty-five and twenty-four years old, respectively, both men displayed this combination of humility and faith to a remarkable degree.

M'Cheyne and Burns also displayed a remarkable degree of humility toward one another, although it would have been quite natural for there to have been jealousy between them. M'Cheyne, the much-beloved pastor, was away from the church when the mighty revival began under the powerful preaching of Burns. His return meant Burns would no longer preach regularly to the people who had quickly come to love him, but there is no evidence of strife between M'Cheyne and Burns. A diary entry by Burns, dated November 22, 1839, describes M'Cheyne's return to Dundee:

> I met Mr. McCheyne at his own house at half-past six, and had a sweet season of prayer with him before the hour of the evening meeting. We went both into the pulpit and after he had sung and prayed shortly, I conducted the remaining services, speaking from 2 Samuel 23:1–5 and concluding at ten. We went to his house together and conversed a considerable time about many things connected with the work of God, and his and my own future plans and prospects.[13]

M'Cheyne would resume his role as pastor at St. Peter's and see a continued work of revival there. Burns would preach throughout Scotland and beyond, seeing much evidence of God's power. Eventually Burns would fulfill his dream of going as a missionary to China, where he would die on April 4, 1868, at the age of fifty-three.[14]

---

13. McMullen, *God's Polished Arrow*, 165.
14. McMullen, *God's Polished Arrow*, 126.

The two Scottish leaders provide valuable lessons for those in the church who wish to see revival today. They teach us that humility comes before power. We must know our utter dependence upon God. We must seek God's power for His glory alone. M'Cheyne and Burns also teach us the need to give preference to others. Revival is not for the purpose of building any individual's reputation, ministry, or church. Leaders must humble themselves before one another, honor each other, and work together toward the common goal of building God's kingdom.

Prepared for Revival

It seems that God prepared M'Cheyne for the revival at St. Peter's by first doing in him what He would later do in the church. God shaped M'Cheyne into a humble man who found endless joy in the message of the gospel. He made him a man of prayer, a person who delighted in fellowship and communion with God. He gave him a love for Scripture and a longing for the cleansing power of the Word to make him more holy. To a significant degree, these are the same things God did in many people when He poured out His Spirit upon the church.

Prayer had been a vital part of the ministry at St. Peter's since the beginning of M'Cheyne's ministry there. The Thursday night prayer meeting had been well attended, and smaller prayer meetings had been encouraged. But when the revival began, many new prayer meetings were formed. Regarding the much-increased emphasis on prayer, M'Cheyne wrote, "At the time of my return from the Mission to the Jews, I found thirty-nine such meetings held weekly in connection with the congregation and five of these were conducted and attended entirely by little children."[15] The love for prayer seen in the pastor was now being seen in the congregation as God poured out His Spirit upon them.

M'Cheyne had faithfully preached and taught God's Word at the church on Sundays, at midweek meetings, and from house

---

15. A. Bonar, *Memoir and Remains*, 544–45.

to house. The people valued his uncompromising proclamation of Scripture. But when the revival came, an entirely new hunger for God's Word was seen. He writes, "The Word of God came with such power to the hearts and consciences of the people here, and their thirst for hearing it became so intense, that the evening classes in the schoolroom were changed into densely crowded congregations in the church, and for nearly four months it was found desirable to have public worship almost every night."[16] The love for God's Word seen in M'Cheyne was now being seen in the church.

An intense pursuit of holiness was evident in M'Cheyne's life well before the revival began at St. Peter's. With the reviving work of God's Spirit, many in the church became aware of their need for cleansing from sin. He wrote, "It pleased God at that time to bring an awfully solemn sense of divine things over the minds of men."[17] Repentance became a hallmark of the revival, and he records, "The effects that have been produced upon the community are very marked."[18] The longing for holiness seen in the pastor was, to a degree, being seen in the people in the church and community.

M'Cheyne's communion with God allowed him to experience God's presence in a way that others would later experience as part of the revival. He lived in such close fellowship with the Lord that his life regularly exemplified the fruit and power of revival. His example teaches us that God prepares in private those he will use in public. Communion with God in prayer, Bible study, and the pursuit of greater holiness and humility will prepare us to be instruments for His power.

Evaluating Revival

M'Cheyne's close personal walk with God prepared him to evaluate the genuineness of the revival that came to Dundee. His high view of God's sovereignty enabled him to respect the extraordinary

---

16. A. Bonar, *Memoir and Remains*, 544.
17. A. Bonar, *Memoir and Remains*, 546.
18. A. Bonar, *Memoir and Remains*, 547.

working of the Holy Spirit during this time. His knowledge of Scripture helped him to discern what was genuine from what was not. His knowledge of revival history was also helpful, as he was able to compare what he was seeing with the experiences of people like Jonathan Edwards.

When an evaluation of the revival at St. Peter's was requested by the Presbytery of Aberdeen, M'Cheyne replied with his *Evidence on Revivals*.[19] His evaluation of the revival was overwhelmingly positive. He wrote, "I am deeply persuaded, the number of those who have received saving benefit is greater than any one will know till the judgement-day." But he also provided an honest assessment of some of the fruit of the revival, noting that "many who came under concern about their souls, and seemed for a time to be deeply convinced of sin, have gone back again to the world."[20] He acknowledged the unusual ways the Holy Spirit had worked among some people, noting, "Sometimes, I believe, He comes like the pouring rain; sometimes like the gentle dew."[21] M'Cheyne expressed his desire for even greater revival by writing, "It is my earnest prayer that we may yet see greater things than these in all parts of Scotland."[22]

M'Cheyne's Example

What can Christian leaders who long to see revival today learn from M'Cheyne's example? First, we should seek a greater working of the Holy Spirit in our own lives. We should seek to know God better and love Him more. Our own communion with God will prepare us to see His greater work in the lives of others.

Second, we should become familiar with how God has worked in past revivals. Church historian Garth Rosell writes that three things have characterized periods of revival throughout the history of Christianity: "These three disciplines—prayer, obedience

---

19. Included in A. Bonar's *Memoir and Remains*.
20. A. Bonar, *Memoir and Remains*, 545–46.
21. A. Bonar, *Memoir and Remains*, 548.
22. A. Bonar, *Memoir and Remains*, 549.

to Scripture and true repentance—have been a central part of every spiritual awakening throughout Christian history and it is likely that this will continue to be true in every future revival until the glorious return of Christ at the end of human history."[23]

Third, we should actively promote prayer for a greater working of the Holy Spirit in our churches, our communities, our nation, and our world. Walter Kaiser has written, "There is no greater work in a revival than the work and ministry of prayer. Without this most necessary petitioning of the Lord, revivals are dead before they get started. This is the universal testimony of all the revivals in the Bible and in history."[24] We should give special emphasis to united, believing prayer, knowing that God has especially used corporate prayer to prepare the way for revival. James Banks notes the impact of corporate prayer in historic revivals and concludes that "praying together changes history."[25]

Fourth, we should present the whole counsel of Scripture without compromise. This means we must be willing to proclaim what the Bible teaches about God's holiness and wrath, the sinfulness of humanity, eternal judgment, and the need for repentance and faith in Jesus. These are foundational teachings of the Bible, yet they are often neglected for fear of offending people. We should heed the wisdom of Martyn Lloyd-Jones, who writes, "The concealing, and the neglect of certain vital truths have always been the chief characteristic of the life of the Church in every period of deadness and of declension." He adds, "No revival has ever been known in the history of churches which deny or ignore certain essential truths."[26] The proclamation of these

23. Kerry L. Skinner, *The Joy of Repentance* (Mobile, Ala.: KLS LifeChange Ministries, 2006), x.

24. Walter C. Kaiser Jr., *Revive Us Again: Biblical Principles for Revival Today* (Geanies House, Scotland: Christian Focus, 2001), 69.

25. James Banks, *The Lost Art of Praying Together* (Grand Rapids: Discovery House, 2009), 16. This is a valuable book for promoting corporate prayer in the local church.

26. Lloyd-Jones, *Revival*, 35.

more difficult doctrines helps to lay the necessary foundation for repentance, and this turning from sin is characteristic of revivals throughout history.[27]

Fifth, we should more consciously honor the presence and power of the Holy Spirit in our lives and in our churches. As Lloyd-Jones writes, "The Church has only one source of strength, and that is the power of God, the power of his Holy Spirit."[28] There must be a desire for the Spirit's power and an embracing of His sovereignty if we are to experience His work in revival. This includes the willingness to allow the unusual without allowing the unbiblical. M'Cheyne reported people sobbing and crying aloud during the revival at St. Peter's. Others were so overcome they could not walk or stand alone.[29] Yet M'Cheyne was discerning enough to recognize that God was genuinely at work. He honored the Holy Spirit, who sometimes "comes like the pouring rain; sometimes like the gentle dew."[30]

Lastly, we must remember that revival is for the glory of God alone. It is not primarily for the purpose of building our churches or improving life in our communities. Revival is for the purpose of magnifying God's holiness and love as the One who is both "just and the justifier of the one who has faith in Jesus" (Rom. 3:26). Knowing Him as our Justifier, we can say with M'Cheyne:

> When this passing world is done,
> When has sunk yon glaring sun,
> When we stand with Christ in glory,
> Looking o'er life's finished story,
> Then, Lord, shall I fully know—
> Not till then—how much I owe.[31]

27. Lewis Drummond, *Eight Keys to Biblical Revival* (Minneapolis: Bethany House, 1994), 91.
28. Lloyd-Jones, *Revival*, 287.
29. A. Bonar, *Memoir and Remains*, 547–48.
30. A. Bonar, *Memoir and Remains*, 548.
31. A. Bonar, *Memoir and Remains*, 636.

Learning from M'Cheyne

- Pray for the Lord to give you a vision and longing for revival in your church and community.

- Pray for a work of revival in your own life. Plan a day apart for personal spiritual renewal.

- Ask God to reveal any sinful pride in your life, recognizing that pride is often the last sin we see in ourselves. Pray the words of Psalm 139:23–24.

- Read a good book on revival history.

Bibliography

Banks, James. *The Lost Art of Praying Together: Rekindling Passion for Prayer.* Grand Rapids: Discovery House, 2009.

Bennett, Arthur. *The Valley of Vision: A Collection of Puritan Prayers and Devotions.* Edinburgh: Banner of Truth, 1975.

Blaikie, William G. *The Preachers of Scotland: From the Sixth to the Nineteenth Century.* 1888. Reprint. Edinburgh: Banner of Truth, 2001.

Bonar, Andrew. *Memoir and Remains of Robert Murray M'Cheyne.* 1844. Reprint. Edinburgh: Banner of Truth, 2004.

Bonar, Andrew, and R. M. McCheyne. *Mission of Discovery: The Beginnings of Modern Jewish Evangelism.* Originally published as *Narrative of a Mission of Inquiry to the Jews from the Church of Scotland in 1839.* Edited by Allan M. Harman. 1839. Reprint. Geanies House, Scotland: Christian Focus, 1966.

Bonar, Horatius. *God's Way of Holiness.* 1864. Reprint. Geanies House, Scotland: Christian Focus, 1999.

———. *The Life of John Milne of Perth.* 1869. Reprint. Edinburgh: Banner of Truth, 2010.

———. *Words to Winners of Souls.* Oradell, N.J.: American Tract Society, 1950.

Bonar, Marjory. *Andrew A. Bonar D. D.: Diary and Letters.* London: Hodder and Stoughton, 1894.

———. *Reminiscences of Andrew A. Bonar D. D.* London: Hodder and Stoughton, 1897.

Bridges, Jerry. *The Discipline of Grace: God's Role and Our Role in the Pursuit of Holiness.* Colorado Springs: NavPress, 1994.

Carson, D. A. *A Call to Spiritual Reformation: Priorities from Paul and His Prayers*. Grand Rapids: Baker, 1992.

Dickson, David and James Durham. *The Sum of Saving Knowledge*. Edinburgh: T and T Clark, 1886.

Drummond, Lewis. *Eight Keys to Biblical Revival*. Minneapolis: Bethany House, 1994.

Edwards, Jonathan. *Heaven: A World of Love*. Edinburgh: Banner of Truth, 2008.

———. *Jonathan Edwards' Resolutions; and Advice to Young Converts*. Edited by Stephen J. Nichols. Phillipsburg, N.J.: P&R, 2001.

Edwards, Jonathan, and Norman Pettit. *The Life of David Brainerd*. New Haven: Yale University Press, 1985.

Gordon, James M. *Evangelical Spirituality*. London: SPCK, 1991.

Haslam, David F. "Robert Murray M'Cheyne (1813–1843)." www. mcheyne.info/rmm.pdf .

Hewat, Kirkwood. *M'Cheyne from the Pew: Being Extracts from the Diary of William Lamb*. London: S. W. Partridge, n.d.

Kaiser, Walter C. Jr. *Revive Us Again: Biblical Principles for Revival Today*. Geanies House, Scotland: Christian Focus, 2001.

The Kneeling Christian. Peabody, Mass.: Hendrickson, 2006.

Lloyd-Jones, Martyn. *Revival*. Wheaton, Ill.: Crossway, 1987.

Loane, Marcus L. *They Were Pilgrims*. Edinburgh: Banner of Truth, 2006.

Lovelace, Richard F. *Dynamics of Spiritual Life: An Evangelical Theology of Renewal*. Downers Grove, Ill.: InterVarsity, 1979.

M'Cheyne, Robert Murray. *A Basket of Fragments*. 1848. Reprint. Geanies House, Scotland: Christian Focus, 2001.

———. *The Believer's Joy*. Glasgow: Free Presbyterian Publications, 1987.

———. *The Cry for Revival*. Three Rivers, U.K.: Diggory, 2007.

———. *Familiar Letters by the Rev. Robert Murray M'Cheyne*. 1848. Reprint. Charleston, S.C.: Bibliolife, 2009.

———. *From the Preacher's Heart*. 1846. Reprint. Geanies House, Scotland: Christian Focus, 1993.

———. *New Testament Sermons*. Edited by Michael D. McMullen. Edinburgh: Banner of Truth, 2004.

———. *Old Testament Sermons*. Edited by Michael D. McMullen. Edinburgh: Banner of Truth, 2004.

————. *The Passionate Preacher: Sermons of Robert M. M'Cheyne*. Edited by Michael D. McMullen. Geanies House, Scotland: Christian Focus, 1999.

————. *Pastoral Letters*. 1844. Reprint. Shoals, Ind.: Kingsley, 2003.

————. "Read the Bible in a Year: Calendar of Daily Readings." 1842. Reprint. Edinburgh: Banner of Truth, 1998.

————. *Sermons of Robert Murray M'Cheyne*. 1961. Reprint. Edinburgh: Banner of Truth, 2000.

————. *Sermons on Hebrews*. Edited by Michael D. McMullen. Edinburgh: Banner of Truth, 2004.

————. *The Seven Churches of Asia*. Geanies House, Scotland: Christian Focus, 2000.

McMullen, Michael. *God's Polished Arrow: William Chalmers Burns*. Geanies House, Scotland: Christian Focus, 2000.

Murray, Iain. H. "Andrew Bonar and Fellowship with Christ." *The Banner of Truth*, no. 156 (December 2010): 8–18.

————. "Robert Murray M'Cheyne: Minister of St. Peter's, Dundee, 1836–1843." *Banner of Truth*. November 12, 2001. http://bannerof-truth.org/us/resources/articles/2001/robert-murray-mcheyne/.

————. *A Scottish Christian Heritage*. Edinburgh: Banner of Truth, 2006.

Owen, John, Kelly M. Kapic, and Justin Taylor. *Communion with the Triune God*. Wheaton, Ill.: Crossway, 2007.

Packer, J. I. *Evangelism and the Sovereignty of God*. Downers Grove, Ill.: InterVarsity Press, 1961.

Piper, John. *Desiring God*. Sisters, Ore.: Multnomah, 2003.

Prime, Derek. *Travel with Robert Murray M'Cheyne*. Leominster, England: Day One Publications, 2007.

Robertson, David. *Awakening: The Life and Ministry of Robert Murray M'Cheyne*. Geanies House, Scotland: Christian Focus, 2010.

Rushing, Richard. *Voices from the Past: Puritan Devotional Readings*. Edinburgh: Banner of Truth, 2009.

Ryle, J. C. *Holiness*. Moscow, Idaho: Charles Nolan, 2001.

Sargent, John. *The Life and Letters of Henry Martyn*. Edinburgh: Banner of Truth, 1985.

Shearer, John. *Old Time Revivals*. Philadelphia: Million Testaments Campaign, 1932.

Skinner, Kerry L. *The Joy of Repentance*. Mobile, Ala.: KLS LifeChange Ministries, 2006.

Smellie, Alexander. *Robert Murray M'Cheyne*. 1913. Reprint. Geanies House, Scotland: Christian Focus, 1995.

Smith, J. C. *Robert Murray M'Cheyne: A Good Minister of Jesus Christ*. 1870. Reprint. Belfast: Ambassador Productions, 2002.

Spurgeon, C. H. *Lectures to My Students*. Peabody, Mass.: Hendricksen, 2010.

Van Valen, Leen J. *Constrained by His Love: A New Biography on Robert Murray M'Cheyne*. Translated by Laurence R. Noculson. Geanies House, Scotland: Christian Focus, 2002.

The Westminster Confession of Faith. Richmond, Va.: John Knox, 1963.

Yeaworth, David Victor. "Robert Murray M'Cheyne (1813–1843): A Study of an Early Nineteenth-Century Scottish Evangelical." PhD dissertation, Edinburgh, 1957.